FAT LUTHER, SLIM PICKIN'S

"Marcia Lane-McGee and Shannon Wimp Schmidt have created something beautiful with this book: offering relevant, hard-hitting, and necessary insights about the Black Catholic experience, providing encouragement to those who want to work toward a more just and fair Church and world, and sharing their genuine hope for all members of the Body of Christ to experience a Church rooted in truth, justice, mercy, and love of the Lord. I've been blessed to call the authors friends for quite some time, and this book is a beautiful snapshot of their personalities, their wisdom, their experiences, and their love for the Church. Anyone lucky enough to pick up this book will be blessed and walk away changed forever."

Katie Prejean McGrady
Host of the *Ave Explores* podcast and *The Katie McGrady Show*
on SiriusXM

"*Fat Luther, Slim Pickin's* rejoices in the beauty of Black culture and bares the hurts and challenges of being Black and Catholic in America. Honest, instructional, and engaging, this intersection of faith and identity celebrates Lane-McGee and Schmidt's heritage and connects us all in our heavenly identity as daughters of the King."

Maria Morera Johnson
Author of *My Badass Book of Saints*

"This thoroughly enjoyable read helps us find provocative, challenging, and hilarious answers to the question, 'What does it mean to be Black and Catholic?' Lane-McGee and Schmidt move us from belly laughs to poignant tears in a vernacular that makes their experiences completely accessible to a wide audience. Their style of writing welcomes me into their lives like a long-time friend who sits at the kitchen counter to discuss important issues and fond memories. Their unique take on life holds up a mirror to our society wrestling to bring an end to racism, sexism, exclusion, and injustice."

ValLimar Jansen
Catholic speaker, recording artist, and storyteller

"Marcia Lane-McGee and Shannon Wimp Schmidt serve up smart, beautifully written reflections about their faith and heritage as fully Black, fully Catholic women. They are honest, humble, funny, gracious, and sometimes—in their own words—even a little weird. I enjoyed not only their engaging stories but also their important, poignant insights. I felt like I've known both of them most of my life. But don't worry, they'll make room for you at the table too. And by the way, the Fat Luther is the better Luther. You'll know what we mean when you read this delightful book."

Gloria Purvis
Catholic radio and television host, author, commentator, and executive producer of *The Gloria Purvis Podcast*

"With a love of both the Church and their cultures, Lane-McGee and Schmidt do a beautiful job of inviting us all into the unique and rich traditions of their faith. This is a book for all of us who are a part of the Catholic family and speaks to the beauty and necessity of diversity in our homes and parish communities."

Erica Tighe Campbell
Founder of Be a Heart

"May this book be your kick in the pants to get on with the hard, and holy, work of doing better."

From the foreword by **Kathryn Whitaker**
Author of *Live Big, Love Bigger*

FAT LUTHER, SLIM PICKIN'S

A BLACK CATHOLIC CELEBRATION
of Faith, Tradition, and Diversity

Marcia Lane-McGee and
Shannon Wimp Schmidt

Ave Maria Press AVE Notre Dame, Indiana

Foreword © 2022 by Kathryn Whitaker

© 2022 by Marcia Lane-McGee and Shannon Wimp Schmidt

Founded in 1865, Ave Maria Press is a ministry of the United States Province of Holy Cross.

www.avemariapress.com

Paperback: ISBN-13 978-1-64680-131-2

E-book: ISBN-13 978-1-64680-132-9

Cover image © www.gettyimages.com

Cover by Kristen Hornyak Bonelli.

Text design by Katherine Robinson.

Printed and bound in the United States of America.

Library of Congress Cataloging-in-Publication Data
Names: Lane-McGee, Marcia, author. | Schmidt, Shannon Wimp, author. |
    Whitaker, Kathryn, other.
Title: Fat Luther, slim pickin's : a Black Catholic celebration of faith,
    tradition, and diversity / Marcia Lane-McGee and Shannon Wimp Schmidt.
Description: Notre Dame, Indiana : Ave Maria Press, [2022] | Includes
    bibliographical references. | Summary: "In this book, Marcia Lane-McGee
    and Shannon Wimp Schmidt speak frankly about their experiences as Black
    women in the Church and invite Catholic women from all walks of life to
    look at the feasts and seasons of the liturgical year through the lens
    of Black Catholic culture"-- Provided by publisher.
Identifiers: LCCN 2021044273 (print) | LCCN 2021044274 (ebook) | ISBN
    9781646801312 (paperback) | ISBN 9781646801329 (ebook)
Subjects: LCSH: Church year--Miscellanea. | Catholic Church--Doctrines. |
    African American women--Religious life. | African American
    Catholics--Religious life. | Catholic women--Religious life.
Classification: LCC BX2170.C55 L26 2022 (print) | LCC BX2170.C55 (ebook)
    | DDC 242/.3082--dc23
LC record available at https://lccn.loc.gov/2021044273
LC ebook record available at https://lccn.loc.gov/2021044274

To D, O, W, M, and M. You are our wildest dreams.

CONTENTS

FOREWORD

Growing up Protestant, I considered the coming of the Spirit at Pentecost one of my favorite Bible passages. The visual of the Holy Spirit descending upon people of all tongues and nations to go forth and preach the Gospel, in whatever way God called them, was powerful. It made me feel as if there was a place for me. Nearly twenty-five years later, now as a confirmed Catholic, I still consider Pentecost one of my favorite Sundays of the liturgical year—reminding me that I belong in the one, holy, catholic, and apostolic Church.

As eloquent as the book of Acts is about people proclaiming the love of Christ, though, nothing about living a Gospel life is comfortable or easy. We often read in scripture where God came to comfort the afflicted and to afflict the comfortable. Just how willing are we to get uncomfortable—to live out the Gospel message and make the table bigger, so to speak?

In this book, Marcia and Shannon walk you through the liturgical calendar, sharing honestly and often vulnerably about their life experiences as women of color. In fact, it was their gracious hearts and willingness to address real issues that touched me the most. Peppered among their stories are features where they dive into Black history, saintly examples, Marian apparitions, and papal encyclicals. Each chapter ends with insightful questions for reflection.

This book made me ask the question: *Do I want a stronger, more faithful and welcoming Church?* And then it convicted me to do the harder task of addressing the seriousness of my *yes*. I couldn't stop at verbal assent—I had to follow through with my actions.

I met Marcia and Shannon online (so 2020, right?), and they introduced me to other Black voices who really challenged beliefs that I, as a white woman, held about race, inclusivity, and belonging. I was drawn to these two women even more when Marcia lost her brother suddenly, shortly after my father's unexpected death, and Shannon wrote a series of poignant articles online. These women made me uncomfortable, but they also made me *curious*. Could I learn more, listen more, do more? How teachable was I allowing myself to be? What a gift it is, to be convicted to act by the experience of others.

In the end, I pray that you see the beauty of their hearts, in their Black glory, and how important it is for men and women of color to have, not just a seat at the table, but a powerful voice, too.

In their introduction, Marcia and Shannon state that through their Black Catholic lens and love of pop culture, they "work to make connections with others and provide a space that fosters listening and learning for people of all backgrounds and belief systems." And they surely did that for me. A priest recently reminded me that we rarely see the mustard seeds we plant come to fruition, but rather we are the beneficiaries of the earnest planting of others. I believe it's time for us to plant seeds of reconciliation, belonging, and love for the harvest of generations to come.

As you read this book, maybe you'll have to google the arguments for Fat Luther versus Slim Luther, or maybe wash day for you has nothing to do with hair. Perhaps you've never personally experienced racism in the Church—but your heart knows that it exists, and you don't know how to confront it. Marcia and Shannon remind us that women are the keepers and preservers of culture. We teach the stories, forge the traditions, prepare the food, and repeat the lessons. How poised are we to bring that strength and wisdom—that "Catholic Shine," as they call it—to fruition in how we treat, welcome, and include others? Maya Angelou often said, "Do the best you can until you know better. Then when you know better, do better." May this book be your kick in the pants to get on with the hard, and holy, work of doing better.

God bless!

Kathryn Whitaker

Catholic convert and author of *Live Big, Love Bigger*

June 19, 2021

INTRODUCTION
Pull Up a Chair

Congratulations! You picked up this book with a weird title (with even weirder authors) ready to learn a bit more about . . . pop culture? Black culture? Catholic culture? All of the above? Well, let us assure you that you're in the right place! Probably.

Before we keep going down this road, let's get to know each other a bit better. I'm Marcia, and my friend Shannon and I make up the dynamic duo behind the premier, international Black Catholic podcast *Plaid Skirts and Basic Black*. It's the place where we look at culture and current events (and whatever other topic we feel like discussing), all through a Black Catholic lens.

WHY *PLAID SKIRTS AND BASIC BLACK*?

We planned to call our podcast *Black and Tan*, which was a tongue-in-cheek reference to both our individual skin tones and our favorite TV show, *Psych*. But upon doing our research we found another podcast had already claimed the name. We were left trying to come up with something that would describe the vibe of our show, and we fixed on the two adjectives we had: Black and Catholic. So "Plaid Skirts" for Catholic school, and "Basic Black" for our blackity-black, bougie basic-ness that loves pumpkin spice, a big fall scarf, and spending way too much money at Target.

It's probably best that we start at the beginning, all the way back in 2004, when Shannon's dad planned a trip to West Virginia with two of his children to spend a week of service with a Catholic outreach organization called Nazareth Farm. He agreed to give me a ride there; at the time I was a super awkward young adult who had no other way to get to the farm for the same event. The whole time we all laughed. We cried. We ate. Then we left and lost touch.

Eight years later, Shannon spied me across a crowded room, telling herself, *No, that's not Marcia. You don't know every other Black Catholic in the world.*

But it *was* Marcia!

And thank goodness I had no qualms giving Shannon a big hug, kickstarting another decade of an incomparable friendship full of kitchen karaoke, meme sharing via text, and a couple of godchildren.

In 2017, we joked that we should start recording the conversations we were having on our daily phone calls. We talked about faith, family, the royal family, our lives, and our roles in the Church, sprinkling in hilarious pop-culture references indiscriminately. It was audio gold. But we are busy people, with busy lives, and we didn't have time or energy to do much outside of our sphere.

A year later, however, we both realized that we'd hit on something important in that flippant aside. In that year, we had found that there was a gap in Catholic media where certain voices were simply left out—Black Catholics, especially Black women, are hard to find.

At this juncture, our podcast was born, ushering in even more important conversations about race, relationships, representation, and royals. Using our Black Catholic lens and love of pop culture, we work to make connections with others and provide a space that fosters listening and learning for people of all backgrounds and belief systems. As Black women, we believe that there is a place for everyone at the proverbial table, and that if there aren't enough seats, we bring in another chair.

This journey through the liturgical year is meant to create some additional space at that table for others to learn. In particular we are here to sit with our fellow Catholics of every background to help us all better understand our culture, our faith, and our hope. We are reserving a special place for our fellow sisters in Christ who may wonder where they belong in our Church. Finally, we incline a nod to our fellow Black Catholics, who are journeying alongside us while leaning on the Lord.

This is our story of how we bring a key piece of who we are—our cultural identity—to our daily lives and to our encounter with Jesus and his Church. It is a glimpse into how we use our history, influences, and all of the blackity-blackness we have to guide us in discipleship. We are so glad you're here with us. But before we get too far ahead of ourselves, back to the introductions. . . .

Introducing Marcia

I've always been the weird kid. I say always because I haven't grown out of it and—being in my early forties—I don't have any plans to do so anytime soon. Once upon a time, I had hope of shedding my weird-kid skin once I found a place to fit in. Yes, I am well aware that I was "born to stand out," but let a girl dream!

So like I was saying, I have always been the weird kid, and that was most true when it came to my faith. At my home church, I didn't sing the gospel music right (I was trained to sing a bit more classically in my school choir); I didn't pray right (too quiet); and I didn't have a ton in common with the other teens because we had all grown up together and they knew how deep my weird went.

To take just one example, the day a classmate at my Catholic junior high discovered that I wasn't Catholic, she was confused and appalled. "You're not Catholic? What's your religion, then?" Nora asked. She was clearly worried I might be a heathen.

"Saved and sanctified!" I responded proudly.

"From what?" she asked, looking at me quizzically. "I don't understand—are you even Christian?"

I didn't know how to answer—or assure her I wasn't following some made-up religion—so I just sat at my desk while she walked around to inform anyone who would listen that I was not Catholic, and my Christianity was TBD.

When my maternal grandmother picked us up from school that day, I knew she would have the answers. "Nannie," I said as I climbed into the front seat of her Chevy Corsica, "how would I know if I am a Christian? I need to tell Nora."

My relief was palpable as she explained that I was, in fact, Christian.

The next day, the determination was radiating from me as I made my way to Nora's desk to let her know what I'd learned the night before.

She just looked at me and said, "Oh, okay," and took the rest of her books out of her bag to settle in for the day. At no point did she make the rounds to absolve me of paganism among my classmates. And I was still weird.

Another eight years would pass before I would find that I actually did fit in and that I had a place in the Catholic Church. I was still weird, but it turns out that I could both fit in and still be the weird kid.

Part of my journey to the Catholic Church and of being a Black Catholic has been embracing my inner weird kid and finding the places where she not only fits, but is also accepted. And now you all are stuck with me.

Introducing Shannon

Whenever I lead a diversity workshop or give a talk about Black Catholic history, I always start with the exact same introduction. It's so routine that I sound a bit like a robot when I repeat it: "Hi, I'm Shannon. I'm biracial. My dad is Black, and my mom is Irish and German."

I make this speech because I have fairly light, olive-toned skin. My hair, though curly, is fine and does not have the distinctive kinks that most people of African descent have. My features favor my mother's Irish family, unlike my siblings, who look much more like my father's side. People have a hard time placing my ethnic heritage when they meet me and generally believe I am a person of European descent. They often wonder why this nice Italian lady is about to talk to them about diversity and Black history.

Even when people know my ethnic background, they often forget that I am not, actually, a nice Italian lady. Once, during my stint as a middle-school theology teacher, I was humorously reminded of this fact.

The school where I worked was very diverse, with significant populations of Black, white, Hispanic, and Asian kids. Every year when I introduced myself to my class, I told them I was biracial and showed them pictures of my family. Since I was one of the only teachers of color and the only person of African descent on the faculty, the Black students often approached me about things that their white teachers didn't understand.

One day, one of my Black students was looking for lotion and, prompted by another Black girl in the class, asked me if I had some. It was wintertime, so I assumed the boy asking for lotion needed it to take care of his dry skin. For most Black people, dry skin is more obvious than it is on a person of European descent; the dead skin cells contrast more on darker skin, often looking like ashes. So in Black culture having dry skin is often referred to as "being ashy."

The two students followed me to my desk, where I located my purse and bent over it to look inside. As I rummaged through it, I asked the boy, "Are you ashy?" I looked up at him as I handed the bottle over. He was tilting his head, staring at me quizzically.

"Mrs. Schmidt," he said with a tone of confusion, "what do you know about being ashy?"

Before I could respond, the girl scoffed at him. "Fool, don't you know she's mixed?"

The poor boy nodded. Suddenly the entire world made sense again. He then proceeded to tell me how I really didn't look like I was Black. I understood his confusion, but I chuckled later at his momentary incredulity at a "white lady" knowing anything about being ashy.

Why "Black" Catholic?

Shannon's mom is Irish. Marcia's mom . . . has an Irish last name. But with two families of Chicago natives, we know that St. Patrick's Day involves so much more than the limited availability of the Shamrock Shake. It is a celebration of the great Irish saint, complete with Irish beer, whiskey, corned beef, cabbage, and soda bread. There's plenty of fanfare to be had throughout the city—the Chicago River is dyed green, we pinch our friends who don't wear the verdant hue, and the whole city turns out for the legendary parade on the South Side.

The year Marcia was preparing to enter the Church, March 17 fell on a Friday. St. Patrick's Day always occurs during Lent, so that meant abstinence from meat on the big day. The Sunday before the feast, while Marcia was attending Mass at St. Columba Church (named, she was told, for the second-greatest saint of Ireland), the priest broke the most important news of the week: the bishop was allowing everyone to eat meat on St. Patrick's Day! The Irish Catholic parishioners cheered and made their way to the butcher to pick up their beef brisket for brining.

Even though it is an Irish and Catholic holiday, St. Patrick's Day is celebrated throughout the whole city by people of every ethnicity and belief system. This specific cultural expression of Catholicism adds to the life and diversity of the whole community—not just the Irish, and not just the Catholics.

We could point out Italian, German, Polish, and Mexican Catholic customs that have also made an impact on the cultural landscape of our hometown as well as many other cultures' traditions. The Church in America is a beautiful mixture of cultures that is hard to find in any other place in the world. Each one enriches the Church as well as the broader American culture.

People of African descent (Africana people)[1] living in the United States have a more complicated cultural landscape than the descendants of the Europeans who immigrated to North America. Africana people in America encompass recent immigrants from Africa, Afro-Latino/a people, and Afro-Caribbean people, as well as African Americans like ourselves. We find all of these people in the Catholic Church, but the term "Black Catholic" does not describe all of them.

When we describe ourselves as Black Catholics, we're not referring to the color of our skin (if that were the case, Shannon would be called a Tan Catholic), but to our cultural heritage as Americans descended from the Africans who were kidnapped from their native lands and forced into labor in the United States. This is a different cultural heritage than that of other Africana people who may be immigrants from African nations, Afro-Caribbean, or Afro-Latino/a.

Unlike people who emigrate from Africa, most of us do not know our nation of origin. Our Afro-Caribbean and Afro-Latino/a brothers and sisters have a unique cultural heritage that is different from our own. When our ancestors were brought to America, their captors purposefully separated family members and those from the same tribes to prevent them from being able to communicate with each other and revolt against their enslavers. Records were erased or purposely obfuscated in order that—even if enslaved peoples were able to free themselves—they would be prevented from tracing their family members or their country of origin. Enslaved Africans therefore had to construct new communities and a new culture with people from every part of Africa. They were called "black" in a new caste system based on a specific biological trait, and it was the only identifier they had to unite them: their skin color.

We, their descendants, now use the word given to us in oppression as a way to describe the unique culture we have created from scratch—a truly American culture that claims Blackness with pride rather than shame and enriches the Church with that culture just as the Irish enrich it with St. Patrick's Day. When we proclaim we are Black Catholics, we are talking not about our race, but about our culture that was forged from nothing into steel.

We live in a country in upheaval from a global pandemic, political polarization, and racial injustice. There is a long road ahead to restore trust and faith in our institutions and in each other. But, as Catholics, we believe that our Church provides the model for how we can live in a diverse, pluralistic America without compromising the values and virtues that advance the common good and uphold the life and dignity of every human person. Our Church embraces every culture and sees the light of Truth in every human community. It encourages us to bring our cultural expressions and our individual gifts and talents to its worship and its proclamation of the Gospel. It does not ask us to conform, but rather, through the guidance of the Holy Spirit, to build unity in diversity.

Diversity: Gift and Calling

Pope Francis points out that, when the Church affirms the value of each cultural expression of the Gospel, it becomes a witness for all people of goodwill. "The experience of a unity that respects and makes room for diversity," he says, "serves as an inspiration and incentive for all those concerned about the kind of world we wish to leave to our children."[2]

Rooted in the Good News of Jesus Christ, and fortified with a wealth of Catholic social teaching, the Church can point a way forward for our nation to find unity in our diversity and bring about the common good. Black Catholics bring a unique gift to this effort. We bring to both our Church and our country the gift of our culture and our history, which offer an essential perspective on the work for racial justice. Our voices provide a framework through which the Church and our nation can begin to address the sin of racism and become more intercultural through embracing diversity, and our voices demonstrate how faith can infuse even the darkest moments with hope.

Our hope in writing this book is that by bringing our voices to the table we will help further that work. While our personal experiences are particular to each of us, we hope that by sharing them and sharing our culture every person can find universal connections to their own life. We hope that as we share our faith it will affirm that of others and, through doing so, we may bless the whole Church.

So pull up a chair. And if there aren't enough, we'll go find one for you.

JANKY LITURGICAL

Preserving Our Culture and Sanity in Advent

Marcia and I love liturgical living. We especially love the rhythms of the Church calendar with its feasts and seasons and the opportunity it gives us to enter into different aspects of the mystery of God's becoming a human being in the person of Jesus of Nazareth.

But as two women who are working full-time, managing households, and trying to keep together some sort of social life, we're usually too exhausted at the end of the day to make something handcrafted for each holiday. In fact, we're far more likely to know the upcoming Starbucks seasonal drink than whatever saint's feast day is coming next.

At my house, for example, there is a beautiful wrought-iron Advent wreath formed in a Celtic knot to pay tribute to my Irish heritage. But last year those lovingly crafted candleholders were filled with the following: one half-used purple candle from the previous Advent; a pristine pink candle that I found in a box full of theology books from college; one of the kids' baptismal candles; and one random white taper that matched the size of the holder. And on St. Nicholas Day—an important festival for my husband Eric's Italian family—I definitely filled the kids' shoes with leftover Halloween candy.

Marcia approaches things a bit differently. When she was managing a residence licensed by the Department of Children and Family Services, candles that could possibly set fire to the house were most definitely out of the question. As a family teacher at a residential school, she didn't always have Catholic youth in the house, so it would have been difficult to make liturgical celebrations a household thing. So for her, celebrating Advent is usually a personal endeavor, done begrudgingly. Marcia's one nod to Advent celebrations entails buying a dress in rose hue every couple of years to wear on Gaudete Sunday. Because on Gaudete Sunday, we wear pink (taking a cue from *Mean Girls* queen bee Regina George—it's important to stay in her good graces, after all). This rather slapdash way of celebrating the liturgical year is what we like to call "janky liturgical."

Normally, *calling* something "janky" is not complimentary. It means that thing probably needs to be fixed or replaced. But *using* something janky means you are making do with what you have and making it work for you. We all have janky things in our lives that are enough to get by for now.

Janky liturgical is messed up and haphazard. It's a little bit fancy and a lot bit frantic. It's making do with what we have so we can do something to mark the Church year because we want to share our faith with others, passing on the traditions that bring our Catholic faith into our homes and our everyday life. It's something we value because we love Jesus and we love liturgy. We're huge fans of the people who make beautiful things to celebrate feasts and seasons. But we're really just not good at crafts. So we love janky liturgical living: anyone can do it. We use what we have on hand and work within our own skill sets to make it work.

Forgot it was Mardi Gras? Buy a sheet cake from the grocery store, stick a plastic toy baby in the middle, hit it with a few sprinkles, and call it a king cake, like I did.

It will look ridiculous. Guests will likely give the cake a hefty dose of side-eye. Kids will complain about how the baby made their piece too crumbly and ask a million questions like, "Why did you steal my baby doll?" or "If I am the Mardi Gras king, can I make Dad clean my room this week?"

But it also provides an opportunity to explain the tradition, why it's important, and what it means, without feeling as if we're going crazy trying to do it all. It's messy, but it's also a moment for sharing the Good News of Jesus Christ.

By focusing on doing something rather than the perfect thing, we give ourselves space to be human. By doing something rather than nothing, we also demonstrate to our family and friends that these special days matter to us and that they have meaning beyond an ordinary day of the year. By marking the days, we make the choice to pass on our faith, traditions, and culture in some way, shape, or form. We create opportunities to open up the mystery of the liturgical year to others, especially to the next generation, and to bring our culture and unique personalities to living our faith in our everyday lives.

Shannon's Story

Advent is my favorite liturgical season. I even got married during Advent because I love it so much. The undercurrents of the season—light, hope, anticipation, watchfulness, waiting—speak to the yearning I feel every December as the days shorten. Preparing for Christmas, I delight in the rich traditions that help us delve more fully into the meaning of the Incarnation.

One of my favorite Advent traditions is the Jesse Tree. As a young child in a Catholic elementary school, I gravitated to the tree where the principal hung ornaments representing important moments and figures in salvation history leading up to the birth of Christ. My eyes would widen as I looked at King David's lyre, Noah's rainbow, and Jacob's ladder. While I didn't totally understand the stories, the visual representation helped me remember them better.

Every day beginning on December 1, a new ornament would appear, a new story would be read, and I would trace its path up the tree toward the place where the ornament representing Jesus would eventually sit. Day by day, I saw the arc of God's work in history make its way closer and closer to Jesus, the One who fully reveals its meaning.

Of course, at age six I didn't really understand that this was what the Jesse Tree was teaching me. But the tradition planted a seed in my heart and in my memory, waiting to bear fruit in its own time.

Now let's fast-forward my story to when I was a twenty-nine-year-old mother of three kids, ages six, three, and two. We were living in a small town in rural Indiana, and to get to the grocery store I had to drive about twenty minutes to the next town north. The most direct route caused us to pass a house flying a Confederate flag and displaying racially charged memorabilia on the front lawn. My shoulders tensed every time it came into view, while I prayed that I would never have to stop at the nearby train tracks for any reason.

Shortly after my oldest son began attending first grade at the local public school, I drove by this house again and decided it was time for our family to have "the talk" about racism. Not because my children are dark-skinned—I have a lighter skin tone and my husband is both German and Italian, so our children look very European. They understand that they have a Black grandfather; that their family is African American and participates in Black culture; even that our ancestors were brought here as part of the slave trade. And though they have largely been spared it themselves, I wanted them to be aware of the discrimination that people with dark skin continue to experience in their everyday lives.

A BLACK HISTORY PRIMER
"ONE DROP" LAWS

The impact of one's skin tone has a long, complicated history for Americans of African descent, dating back to the slave codes enacted in the colonial period. At the time the first enslaved Africans were brought to Virginia in 1619, Africans were treated like other indentured servants from Europe. After a certain period of service or for a certain amount of money, they would be considered free citizens in the colonies. They were also allowed to bring complaints against their masters to the courts if they felt they were being unjustly treated.

This changed in 1705 when the Virginia General Assembly passed the *Act Concerning Servants and Slaves*. The act stated that any person who was not Christian in their native land was enslaved for the entirety of their life unless they were manumitted by their masters, and that any children born to an enslaved woman kept her status for their lifetime. Slaveholders no longer faced any legal culpability for the methods used to punish the enslaved, either, including punishment by death.

Similar laws were passed throughout the Southern colonies, codifying the legal status of multiracial people as "black" and allowing their continued enslavement no matter what they looked like, or whether they had European ancestry. The language usually stated that a person was to be classified as a slave if they had "even one drop of Black blood." It was a way to prevent descendants of African people from gaining power or wealth, or even reclaiming their freedom.

The "one drop" language is still used today by groups that hold racist and white supremacist views, and who use symbols like the Confederate flag and caricatures of African Americans and Hispanic Americans to degrade and intimidate Black and

Brown people—not unlike the treatment that the Jews received in Nazi Germany.

Americans of African descent know that skin color doesn't automatically protect a person from intimidation, discrimination, or harm. This is why, for our families, it is a matter of survival to make our children aware of these attitudes and symbols as they make their way through the world.

||||||||||||||||||||||||||||||||||||||||||||||||||||||||||||||||||||||||||||||||||||||||||||||||||||||||||||||||||||||||||||||||||||||||||||||||||||||||||||||||||||||||||||||||||||

When Eric and I sat down to discuss the house flying the Confederate flag with our son, I had a clear outline in my head of how the conversation would flow. We would talk about the flag and what it stood for, about words for Black people that were never to be used, and about the importance of caring for people of every background.

I began to explain to my son about some of the racist language people used for people of African descent. He seemed to follow what I was saying, though he was slightly confused about why I wanted to tell him about it. When I started to say what he should do if he ever heard anyone using racially charged insults, he turned quizzically to me. "But why would they say things like that to me, Mom?"

Before I could respond, my husband jumped in. "Because you're Black."

My son shot Eric a look of complete confusion. He rapidly looked down at his very light olive skin, then looked back at Eric as if he had two heads.

"Well, Grandpa is Black," Eric continued, "so you're Black."

"But my skin is white!" our son replied, as if his father had suddenly lost his mind or perhaps his ability to see color.

I slapped my palm to my forehead and laughed. "What Dad means is that your family is African American, buddy. That our ancestors came from Africa and they were slaves." Looking pointedly at my husband, I added, "I would have said that we are people of African descent."

Eric shrugged playfully, feigning bewilderment.

"Well, I knew that!" my son replied. "Is that why people would say mean things to me?"

"Yes, it is," Eric replied, going on to discuss what to do if any situation should come up.

When our son went back to playing with his siblings, I shook my head at my husband in mocking chastisement, and he responded with a good-natured grin.

"Maybe next time leave the Black stuff to me, white man," I said, winking.

This story illustrates how important it is for Eric and me to be intentional about how we teach our children. It shows why passing on our traditions requires work and deliberate effort. The way we talk to our children—especially the stories that we tell about who our family is—is an important way to preserve and pass along the traditions of our cultures to them. In our house, we believe it's extremely important to work at preserving and honoring our cultures.

How else will they know their African American (or German, or Irish, or Italian) culture unless I choose to pass it on to them? So we make a special effort to expose them to Black history as well as African American food, music, books, and movies. We spend time in predominantly Black neighborhoods, at Black events, and in Black spaces so they can see what my culture is like and feel comfortable within it. Even if they will be seen as white, they can still be proud to be African Americans and to lift up the culture for future generations. I teach them these things so that they know who they are and where they came from.

The same can be said about our Catholic faith. Traditions have to be passed on. The stories we tell from scripture, the saints, and our own lives are what bring the living history of the People of

God into the next generation. This is why every Advent our family puts up a Jesse Tree.

It all started one Sunday morning after religious education class. My children, who attend public schools, were trying to tell me what they had learned about the faith that day when it hit me that they really didn't know the Bible that well. Not, like, memorizing passages from Paul's letters and reciting them, but simple stories about Creation, Noah's ark, Joseph's coat, and the Exodus. Even though we went to Mass every week and were involved at our church, something wasn't sticking. They didn't have Catholicism woven into their school day like I did.

I knew we had to do something to help them, and suddenly that seed blossomed: the Jesse Tree. Those stories that had captivated me were right there, waiting to be learned.

So now, every Advent, we pull out our Jesse Tree ornaments and hang them. (I bought the ornaments online. I didn't make them. And half of them have crayon scribbles on them now . . . janky liturgical.) We read the scripture passage related to each story. (Or sometimes I paraphrase it because the kids are really squirmy and think the Bible is boring . . . janky liturgical.) Sometimes, we even talk about where they see God in the story. (Or everyone starts wrestling and we pretend it's a reenactment of Jacob wrestling with God . . . janky liturgical.)

We are not very good at liturgical living at my house. We have to work at it. Most days we're so tired we'd rather forget it. My four young kids run through the house with reckless abandon, never pick up their clothes from the floor, and complain on their way to religious education each week. I've accidentally fed everyone chicken nuggets on a Friday in Lent and rolled my eyes in frustration at the priest who gave a thirty-minute homily while my toddler screamed bloody murder in the cry room. I'm a normal Catholic mom who sometimes wonders if my kids' baptisms took the first time.

But unless Eric and I do something to pass on our traditions and our faith, our kids won't absorb it from the world. We can't take for granted that they'll know Jesus if we don't invite them to meet Jesus. If we want them to see what discipleship looks like—to feel comfortable in it—then they have to see us trying to be disciples. They will only know what it means to be Christian if we teach them who they are and to whom they belong.

So—even if it means we're stumbling out of the car in mismatched sweatpants to get to Ash Wednesday Mass on time—we do our best to expose them to faith traditions, to share what our own faith means to us. Janky liturgical works for us because it gives the Holy Spirit room to work in our house.

And here's the thing: the Holy Spirit doesn't care if your Advent wreath is made from four tiny birthday candles you found at the bottom of a drawer. The Spirit will come as long as you make room.

Marcia's Story

Unlike Shannon, I don't consider Advent my favorite season. Since I wasn't raised Catholic, I didn't celebrate Advent growing up. It wasn't until I encountered the bombastic celebration of the liturgical seasons during my seventh-grade year at St. Gertrude's School that I discovered there was more to Advent than just buying presents and making treats for Christmas.

The Advents of my childhood revolved around church. My mom was the head of our Sunday school's entertainment committee. This meant that she was in charge of preparing for all of the holidays and organizing all of the social activities. As her children, my sisters and I were "volun-told" to help her. She worked hard, pulled off some great events, and managed to break only a *few* child-labor laws in the process.

I spent the weeks before Christmas learning lines for a Christmas pageant, attending choir rehearsal, or doing whatever else I had to do to aid my mom in service of our church. My baby sister

Joey had it easy. She was the angel every year. I mean, sure, she was adorable, but I think it had more to do with the fact that my family owned the costume than her precociousness. So, as long as she could fit in it, the gig was hers. Every year when December hit, our house would ring out in a cacophony of disjointed Christmas tidings, punctuated by a shrill, "Fear not, Mary!"

Advent was also a time of stress and struggle for my family. My sisters, mom, and I were often reminded of what we didn't have and what we couldn't get. My sisters and I had absent fathers; Mom was our sole provider. Advent was sometimes a period when we had to go without. Even though we were active making magic happen for our church community, we never let on that, after the Christmas pageant wrapped up, we would pack up the car (angel costume included!) and drive home across town in a car with no heat, to arrive at a house that might not have heat either. Or electricity. Or food. There were also times when we didn't actually have a place to call home.

As I grew older, I came to realize that my mom's added stress during this season came from trying to figure out how to provide a good Christmas for us on top of just needing to provide. In eighth grade I started volunteering at the parish food pantry. Other classmates were there to complete service hours for Confirmation preparation, and I decided to join them. I learned that most of the volunteers were also clients, and that they were able to take a bag of food home after a shift. From then on I volunteered as often as I could through my senior year in high school, every time bringing home a bag of groceries to help my mother provide for our family.

At sixteen, I stopped giving my mom a Christmas list. It was hard to watch her work for years while barely managing to make ends meet. Seeing her struggle even more to make Christmas happen was even harder. I remember observing my mom that Christmas as my sisters opened their gifts, wrapping paper flying around them. Mom looked exhausted, even though her eyes reflected her happiness at their delight. I stood up to start cleaning the wrapping paper from the floor, when she realized I had only received a pair of gloves to match the coat she'd given me for my birthday three days earlier.

"Marci," my mom said. "Did I not get you anything? Did you give me a list?"

My sisters suddenly stopped admiring their gifts.

"No," I answered sheepishly, "I couldn't think of anything I wanted this year."

Mortified, my normally unflappable mother started apologizing and didn't stop until the following week.

From then on, my mom made a production of asking for my Christmas list each December. We began to tell and retell that story at our family Christmas celebrations, accompanied by gasps and laughter. The story soon took its place in our family lore. And from that day on, everyone "knew" that I really didn't care about Christmas gifts, that I was hard to shop for, and that I always buy the things I like for myself anyway.

The good news is that as the years passed, whether we were in a season of feast or famine, I didn't have to worry about whether my presents were a burden for my mother. I didn't feel that I was contributing to her exhaustion, and I could still experience Christmas joy with my family each year.

Advent is supposed to help us focus on the virtues of hope, peace, joy, and love as we look forward to the excitement of Christmas. I didn't experience much hope, peace, joy, and love as a teenager living at or below the poverty line. Waiting on the Lord during Advent hits a little harder when you've always been waiting.

In the twenty-five years since I "forgot" my Christmas list, I've never forgotten what it is like to wait so profoundly and seemingly without end. Almost every time we start a new liturgical year, I'm reminded of that teenager who had to do her homework by the candlelight of an Advent wreath, desperately trying to hold on to hope; find peace despite our situation; and remember that joy often comes after a night of weeping, loving the Lord through it all.

Advent is the time when I am reminded of my journey, and how far I have come. With maturity I can now embrace the waiting because—while I didn't love the struggle—I can appreciate the lessons.

Because of my own experience, Advent is a season when I feel called to serve and celebrate the dignity of those most in need in a special way. My mother gave me her heart for service, and when added to the treasure of Catholic social teachings, it has helped me to be a cheerful giver in giving the poor what, ultimately, belongs to them: the goods of the earth that God has created. There are many people who, just like sixteen-year-old Marcia, have a hard time waiting on an infant Savior while they're in line to get their basic needs met. I just make sure they don't have to wait alone or wait too long.

Service aside, I still don't think I celebrate a very "Catholic" Advent. I don't have a wreath. I always have to look up the themes for weeks two and four. And I only just learned about the existence of the St. Andrew novena last year. I still help my mom at the Protestant church of my youth, spending the days before Christmas leading a new generation in the ways of the pageant—and, of course, fitting another little girl for an angel costume. My janky celebrations are my own. They might not be pretty, but they work for me. Besides, I like buying that new pink dress.

Making Do and Making Room

What our two stories have in common is the willingness to be open to whatever God has in store for us, even if it's not wrapped in a beautiful bow. We've discovered that God shows up, even if we have to wait and even if we have to make room for the Spirit to move. In whatever ways we can, we try to stand before the Lord with open hands and open hearts ready to receive him.

The beauty of the life of discipleship is that, before we even know God or offer anything in return, mercy and grace are offered to us. The Holy Spirit is poured out upon us through the sacraments regardless of our worthiness or openness. That's one of the reasons we baptize infants in the Church. God gives us the Spirit simply because he loves us and wants to draw us into the divine life of love.

Advent is a time to meditate on the mystery of God's willingness to redeem us and to see the movement of the Holy Spirit both in salvation history and in our own lives. It reminds us that the only posture God asks of us is openness. By standing with open hands and hearts before the Lord, we can see the marvelous things the Spirit has done and will continue to do for God's people.

Being Catholic is not about being perfect—it's about cooperating with God's grace and being willing to make the best out of what we have to offer. Sometimes our discipleship looks a little janky because it's what we can work with, rather than what we would like to give God. We make do with what we have because it works for us and—more importantly—through it God works wonders for us.

AN ADVENT COMPANION
SARAH THE MATRIARCH

Sarah, the wife of Abraham, first appears in Genesis 12 as a relatively young and beautiful woman, full of faith and trust in her husband and in the God who called him from their home to a new land. As they travel, she is desired by kings and becomes the matriarch of a large, prosperous tribe. But even as God blesses Abram with prosperity, he does not bless Sarah with the long-awaited child she hopes to conceive. She begins to lose faith in

God's promise, to grow bitter with disappointment, and to believe that God will never end her waiting.

When Sarah takes matters into her own hands, she creates a mess. She offers Hagar as a concubine to Abraham, resulting in the birth of Ishmael. When Sarah herself finally gives birth to Isaac, her jealousy and anger create a rift between the two brothers, and between herself and Abraham. Her anger ultimately endangers the lives of Ishmael and Hagar before God intervenes for their safety. Sarah learned the hard way that when we don't offer God what we have, when we try to make things perfect by our own standards, our plans go awry.

Yet Sarah found her faith again. It's quite possible that Abraham informed her of God's request that he offer their son as a sacrifice. If so, she watched Abraham and Isaac leave with the wood of the sacrifice meant for her son without complaint. Her lack of action shows a trust, perhaps hard-won, in God's faithfulness to fulfill his covenant and bring her only son back to her. She was willing, this time, to wait on the Lord's action instead of undertaking her own.

Sarah is our Advent companion because she was not perfect. She made mistakes yet learned from them and offered God what she had in trust, believing that God could—and would—be faithful in return.

REFLECTION **QUESTIONS**

1. What are some ways that you celebrate different parts of the liturgical year in your home? Are your celebrations pretty and planned to the last detail, or are they more like Shannon and Marcia's versions of janky liturgical living? Or a little of both?

2. Shannon talks about the importance of working to preserve and pass on her African American heritage to her children. How do you make time to share your cultural traditions?

3. Marcia discusses how Advent has not always been a time of happy anticipation for her. Have there been moments in your life when a trial has tempered your celebration of the liturgical seasons?

4. Do you have any favorite Advent traditions? Why are they important to your celebration of the season?

5. The chapter concludes by reminding us to be open to the movement of the Holy Spirit. What is one concrete way you can make more room for the Spirit's movement in your day-to-day routine?

"WHAT ARE YOU?" AND OTHER RUDE QUESTIONS

Walking with Our Lady of Guadalupe

Our Lady of Guadalupe is a G.

Before we continue, some explanations may be in order. If you don't know what a G is, you're probably like, "Duh! 'Guadalupe' begins with the letter G!" While that may be true, that's not why Our Lady is a G. Of all the explanations we have to offer in this book, this one is the hardest. It's one of those terms that if you know, you know, and if you don't, the understanding comes with experience. This is where Shannon's teacher voice and my street smarts come into play . . . we'll do our best.

The term "G" is short for "gangsta," which is short for . . . "gangster." Whether your mind wanders to Chicago with the likes of Al Capone and John Dillinger or to Los Angeles with the Bloods and the Crips, you have a good idea. (Stay with us, people; we do not believe Our Lady resembles in any way, shape, or form gangsters and the violent lives they lead!) And yet, there is one surprising point of commonality: their desire to provide for and protect those they cared about. Though these men did unethical things and made immoral decisions, they started out being laser focused on providing for and protecting their own communities. These men meant business and were about their business.

So the term "gangster" was eventually shortened to "gangsta," and later to "G." But the meaning of the term continued to evolve. While it originally had connotations of violence revolving around gang life in the inner city (in any era), eventually calling someone a G became a term of respect in Black culture. Calling someone a G has nothing to do with the life they lead, but rather it is used to praise their character. Nowadays the term "G" is used to describe someone who is considered admirable because, despite the unkindness of life, they have maintained their strength and courage. It is someone to whom everyone will listen and give respect because they're known for having a certain gravitas and command of a situation. A G doesn't pull any metaphorical punches and gets things done. "G" is a title reserved for men, women, and apparitions who do the same.[1]

Now that you understand what we mean, don't you agree? From this moment on, the Marian apparition that appeared on Tepeyac will be known as "OLG the G."

So why do we call Our Lady of Guadalupe a G? We need to look at her story and its meaning to better understand.

A BLACK HISTORY PRIMER
APPRECIATION VS. APPROPRIATION

Learning about different cultures leads to understanding, acceptance, and interest. When this learning is done in earnest, we can appreciate what other cultures bring to the table and how their contributions broaden our perspective and shape a more diverse worldview. As a people, we can use that appreciation to unite us. Appropriation, on the other hand, seeks to broaden the divide.

Appropriation, specifically cultural appropriation, occurs when an individual or culture uses objects and/or elements of another culture in a way that ultimately diminishes their meaning, lessens respect, omits credit to the source, reinforces long-held stereotypes, and contributes to oppression. By taking the symbols and goods of another culture and using them for purposes for which they were not intended, we deprive them of their meaning and exploit the richness of other human beings' creativity and wholeness. In some ways, cultural appropriation reveals our own unwillingness to do the hard work of intercultural relations, even when it is not our intention.

Cultural appropriation is easy to slip into when we do not commit to earnestly learning about and appreciating diverse cultures. Everyone can be guilty of appropriation, including the two of us. We have both used the term "spirit animal" to express our affection for a person, place, or thing, trivializing the deeply important meaning of that term for Native American spirituality and familial ties. And—once upon a time—one of us (cough, Marcia) thought it was *so cool* to get the Chinese symbol for "truth" tattooed on her body. Let our behavior serve as a learning experience, a cautionary tale, and a reminder that when we know better, we are more likely to do better.

We can avoid cultural appropriation by engaging in significant and consistent encounters with people in a specific culture. We can ask about the meaning of objects, art, phrases, and symbols from many people of that culture, especially those considered cultural stewards. By asking those within the culture what is acceptable for those outside the culture to use, we can avoid use of objects that are not meant for our consumption. So, for example, if you're on vacation in Senegal and want to buy fabrics for your home, buy them from Senegalese merchants who can direct you to fabrics that are appropriate for such use. Or, in the United States, make purchases from Ethical Trade merchants, who are connecting consumers to craftspeople directly from specific cultures. By purchasing from these communities themselves or from sources that directly benefit those communities, we not only avoid misuse of cultural items, but we also avoid the exploitation of their labor and encourage continued flourishing of their cultures.

Our Lady of Guadalupe is one of those symbols of Mexican culture that we can appreciate, but should not appropriate by removing her from her cultural context—which we do when we casually or thoughtlessly use her image in ways that contradict the message of her apparition. Rather, taking time to understand what she means to Mexican culture helps us better understand who Mary is and how this apparition speaks to us in our culture and our own time.

So, to sum up, buy that souvenir, but don't get Chinese writing inked by a white dude in a Chicago tattoo parlor. Please don't let Marcia's permanent facepalm be in vain.

La Virgen de Guadalupe

Ten years after the Spanish conquest of the Aztec people in Mexico, a poor Aztec man named Juan Diego was walking past Tepeyac Hill in December to go to church when he heard birds singing and a woman calling out to him by name. Upon climbing the hill, he was greeted by the Blessed Virgin Mary, who asked him to go to the bishop and request that a church be built on the hill where she stood.

Juan Diego asked the bishop multiple times to fulfill Our Lady's request, but the bishop refused. He told Juan Diego that he would not build the church without a sign from God. When Juan Diego next spoke with Our Lady, she told him to gather roses that were growing on the hill. Not only were the roses blooming miraculously in December, but they were Castilian roses from Spain—flowers that did not belong in Mexico at all.

Juan Diego gathered the flowers in his tilma, a coarse baggy garment used by peasants, and took them to the bishop. Upon releasing the roses onto the bishop's floor, Juan uncovered an image of the Blessed Virgin as she had appeared to him on the hill, miraculously imprinted on the tilma. The bishop hung the tilma in his chapel and began construction on the church, which would become the Basilica of Our Lady of Guadalupe. The tilma, which is almost five hundred years old, still hangs there without any decay, preserving the image of Our Lady for generations of new believers.

Mother of a New People

Everything about Our Lady of Guadalupe has meaning. To put the apparition in context, when she appeared to Juan Diego in December 1531, the Aztec people were possibly at their lowest. Their tribes had been conquered by Spain. Almost half of the population had been wiped out by smallpox, a disease brought to the continent by the Spanish to which the native population had no natural immunity. They would have seen their defeat by the Spanish as proof that the new strange God of their conquerors was more powerful than all of their gods. By their cultural standards, the new colonizers, in winning the war, had every right to rule their lands.

It was at this moment in Mexico's history that Our Lady appeared to Juan Diego, speaking Nahuatl (the indigenous Aztec language) and looking mixed race in appearance. She was clothed as one from the Spanish aristocracy but arrayed in Aztec and Christian symbols. She did not come to the conquerors, but rather to the conquered, signifying God's nearness to them and their inherent dignity in the eyes of Christ—contrary to what their culture told them to believe about who God favors.

Our Lady drew from both the Aztec and Spanish cultures to convey truths about Christ and to point to a new cultural identity that was uniquely Mexican.

SYMBOLS OF LA VIRGEN

The apparition of Our Lady of Guadalupe is rich in symbols and meaning.[2] Here is just some of the significance behind the image found on the tilma:

Mary's appearance blends aspects of both Spanish and Aztec culture. Our Lady wears the clothing of Spanish nobility and a golden cross, but looks like a "mestiza" (a darker mixed-race woman). Tepeyac Hill, where Mary appeared, was the site of a temple to the Aztec goddess Tonantzin, the mother goddess. The blue-turquoise color of her mantle was also associated with Tonantzin, symbolizing deity, royalty, and fertility. However, unlike the images of Aztec gods who would stare directly at the viewer, Mary's eyes are turned downward in humility, signifying her human nature.

Similarly, the various symbols in the image are drawn from both Christian and Aztec religious iconography. Around Mary's waist is a bow, a symbol of virginity, but she is visibly pregnant. The pregnant woman clothed with the sun, standing on the moon, and crushing the serpent directly recalls the woman of Revelation 12 in the Christian tradition. To an Aztec viewer, however, the rays of the sun would be seen as a symbol of the highest god, Huitzilopochtli, and the moon a symbol of the god of night. Mary's position in front of the sun and on top of the moon shows that she announces a God more powerful than both. In addition, she is carried by angels, which was a mark of royalty in Aztec culture, but would also be familiar to Christians.

Our Lady's apparition is a divine work of *inculturation*—that is, the expression of the universal truths of our Catholic faith through the unique symbols and customs of an individual culture.

Inculturation is the way in which the light of the Gospel both transforms a culture and is understood in new ways because of its encounter with a new culture. Take, for example, the celebration of Halloween and Día de los Muertos. Both are cultural celebrations of All Saints' Day and All Souls' Day—feasts of the universal Church. But each is unique in its emphasis on shared Catholic themes.

Halloween, brought to the world from Ireland, pokes fun at evil. We dress up like ghouls and ghosts to show that those things have no power over us because of Christ's victory over sin and death. Día de los Muertos, on the other hand, welcomes the dead as old friends, keeping the stories of loved ones alive, acting as a living witness to our belief in the Communion of Saints and the thin veil that separates us from those who live forever in Christ. Both holidays recognize that sin and death are ultimately no match for Jesus, but the unique traditions of the Irish and Mexican people on display express that belief in particularly Mexican and Irish ways.

The work of inculturation is not new in the Church. We can see traces in scripture as the apostles traveled the Roman Empire and decided that Gentiles need not convert to Judaism (or be circumcised) in order to be baptized. We also see it in the early Church, which began to adopt parts of Roman culture to order its worship (influencing its architecture, vestments, and rituals).

Our Lady of Guadalupe is like a divine blueprint for what inculturation should be. Using both Spanish and Aztec religious symbols—even a site of Aztec worship—she reveals truth through images, words, and expressions that the people would understand. She does not negate either culture, but rather transforms both and reveals their true meaning in Jesus.

The apparition exemplifies the instructions of Pope St. Gregory the Great to Abbot Mellitus, a missionary to Britain. Gregory encouraged adapting pagan customs to illustrate the truth of Christianity and reconsecrating pagan shrines to Christ, so that "seeing that their temples are not destroyed, may remove error from their hearts . . . knowing and adoring the true God."[3] This is, quite literally, what Our Lady of Guadalupe did by appearing to Juan Diego.

Our Lady of Guadalupe is a G because she brings the love of God to people who are desperate. With a mother's strength, she did not give in when the bishop challenged the validity of Juan Diego's story. Instead she interceded with God to bring about miracles that upended the expectations of those in power. Her intervention was so powerful that La Virgen de Guadalupe became a central unifying image of Mexican identity. She became the mother of a whole new people.

However, we are not Mexican (as far as we know). So, what exactly does Our Lady of Guadalupe mean to us?

Shannon's Story

My least favorite question in the world is probably, "What are you?"

I know what the question is asking—"What is your ethnic identity?"—but it comes across as someone asking whether or not I am actually human.

Humans—because our brains like order and classification—have a hard time dealing with information that does not fall into our preconceived notions about life. Because of what I call my "vaguely ethnic" appearance, I am often met with confusion by people of all backgrounds as they try to place where I belong in the brain's schema when it comes to race and ethnicity.

Unfortunately this impulsive quest for orderliness often prompts blunt questions that border on rudeness (however unintentional). Here is a small sampling:

"But really, how black is your dad?"
"Are your parents married?"
"Where is your family really from?"
"Why don't you just say you're white?"

I've learned not to react in anger to these questions. Most of the time, people are trying to give voice to their jumbled thoughts and learn more about me. More often than not, I may be the first multiracial person they have met and—as with all diversity work—it's best to assume that people have good intentions in order to come to common ground and mutual trust.

But that wisdom has been hard-won for me. As a child and young adult, I frequently felt like a unicorn—too white for black spaces and too black for white spaces—and I felt I had to make a choice to be one or the other to be accepted. If I chose to embrace one culture, at least I would have a firm cultural identity. I would be just Irish or just German or just African American like everyone else.

There was also a temptation to throw off my cultural heritage and embrace something entirely new. When I studied in Rome during my college years, I found myself drifting into this sort of denial. Since I look like most Mediterranean people, I could blend in, and I immersed myself in the culture by trying to look and act like a native Italian whenever I could get away with it. When someone reacted with surprise on finding out that I was American, I would glow with pride.

What cured me of this cultural shape-shifting was Chinese food. After two or three months of eating only Italian food, I was craving something different. I wanted a cheeseburger, some ribs, or tacos al pastor. My taste buds had been spoiled by the cultural landscape of American cuisine, which combines so many flavors from every continent, and I was fed up (no pun intended) with only eating Italian food.

So when one of my classmates announced he had discovered a Chinese restaurant a short walk from our school, I jumped at the offer to join him. We gathered a small group of friends for a multi-course dinner, rejoicing when the tangy soy sauce hit our lips. We laughed heartily, reveling in the familiar tastes and smells, talking about the things we missed in the United States—even though none of us would have traded our time in Rome for a plane ticket back. We meandered home along the uneven cobblestones in the crisp spring air of the Eternal City, smiling in gratitude for a small reminder of the best of our multicultural American society.

Lying in my bed that night, I felt bittersweet tears trickle silently down my face. I loved Italy, but I missed home. And I recognized that I was missing out on so much of what I loved about myself by trying to ignore my unique cultural heritage. As comfortable as I was in Italian culture, it was something that could become a part of me without replacing what was already there. To ignore one part of my cultural heritage for another or to try to take on an entirely new one did not nourish my soul, nor did it draw me closer to the God who made me to be exactly who I am.

I am the descendant of Irish peasants who came to America seeking a better way of life. I am the descendant of German Catholics who brought their love for their faith to the Midwest. I am the descendant of enslaved Africans who forged a new culture when it seemed as if they had nothing left. I am all of these things, and I can embrace each of these things without losing any of the others.

That willingness to embrace a new intercultural reality is what I see reflected in Our Lady of Guadalupe. La Virgen affirmed the best of both Aztec and Spanish cultures, using the symbols of both to point to a new Mexican identity. She spoke to a man who felt lost, downtrodden, and as if he had lost his culture, showing him that God cares for him and for his people. They did not have to relinquish their cultural identity in order to draw closer to God. Most importantly, Our Lady's appearance reveals that the true meaning of who the Mexican people would become is found in the Good News of Jesus Christ. It is the Gospel that can bring peace and reconciliation to two peoples in conflict and give them a common hope for the future.

Our Lady of Guadalupe teaches me that the fullness of all cultures is found in Christ, in whom we can find a way forward to celebrate what we hold in common without denying what makes us distinctive and unique. Our Lady is a model of how to overcome the anger, bitterness, and disappointment of the past and look to the future in hope. It's no accident that she is the Mother of the Americas. We need a mother who can help our culturally diverse nation forge a way beyond our contentious past.

Our Lady also teaches me the Church's role in my life. It is a place where I can be affirmed in my individuality and my diverse cultural heritage. It is also a place in which I can encounter new cultures and appreciate the ways they enrich my understanding of who God is and what it means to be human.

As we'll discuss in later chapters, women have an important part to play in helping diversity flourish in the Church. As a woman trying to impact the Church and the world for the better, I can't find a better role model than the Virgin of Guadalupe. Through her apparition she changed Mexico forever. Our Lady is a woman who got things done.

But that doesn't surprise me in the least. After all, Our Lady of Guadalupe *is* a G.

Marcia's Story

Growing up, I spent a lot of time with my grandparents. Their influence shows in my mannerisms and turns of phrase, and I still hold on to some of their habits. One that has always stuck with me is "not sitting on my bed with my street clothes," both literally and figuratively. While I may have to shove over a week's worth of clean laundry, among other things, to settle in for the night, I am not bringing anything unclean, unsafe, or unwelcome into that space by wearing my "street clothes." Our beds are supposed to be the safest place we know. For me, it is the place I can let my guard down without any preamble. In my pajamas and nestled in between my Star Wars sheets and my old-school He-man blanket, I allow myself to rest and recharge. The nights when I happen to fall into bed with the day's clothes on, I feel less ready to face the morning. In order to protect my peace and, in many ways, my spiritual health, I have to create that boundary with myself. I also have to set this boundary in my relationships with others.

No, I do not make people bring a change of clothes when they come over to my home for dinner, but I do make sure they come into my space and my life with clean intent. Vulnerability is hard for me, specifically vulnerability in areas I haven't yet worked through, and depending on where and how you find me, I can sometimes be a bit . . . prickly. When and if I let you into my space, I have to be able to trust that your intent isn't to disrupt my peace. And you need to be open to my telling you the impact your actions have. Please don't sit on my bed with your street clothes on.

I'm not sure where I heard the term or if I made it up, but I often tell people that I have been navigating whiteness since I was twelve years old. If you remember, that is around the same time my seventh-grade class believed me to be pagan, and I learned on many levels that I was different from my classmates. My differences made me stick out in ways that I found uncomfortable, and I worked hard to fit in with my peers. Oftentimes I had to sacrifice being understood and accepted (an exhausting feat) in order to be one of the gang and not merely tolerated. Because I (inadvertently) chose the latter for most of my formative years, I rarely got a good night's sleep, and I didn't feel comfortable in my own skin for a long time. I worked so hard to find acceptance that I would row my boat to any given shore and mold myself to impossible expectations of assimilation and whiteness while allowing, and believing, false and toxic narratives about my hair, skin, body, and background.

I learned the story about Our Lady of Guadalupe the day after I came into the Church. I was at a friend's house for Easter, and I commented on an image I recognized from the *panadería* (or Mexican bakery) in my neighborhood.

"You have a Mexican Mary!" I said to my friend and his family.

"Umm . . . that's Our Lady of Guadalupe." He looked at me like I had three heads. "Do you know the story?"

I didn't. So I gave it my best shot. "Well, I had a friend in third grade named Guadalupe—we called her Lupe. Like that?"

That, it turns out, was not sufficient. Ed and his siblings were incredibly animated when telling me the story of the woman who appeared to Juan Diego and the miracles proceeding from that encounter. It turns out that my understanding that "Mexican Mary" was like having a Black Jesus was completely off base. The framed (or velvet) photos of Black Jesus in our grandparents' homes or the corner store were meant to represent a Savior that came to free us, and as a direct contradiction to the consistently white-skinned Jesus to which we were accustomed. Our Lady of Guadalupe, I would come to learn and ponder over, wasn't a representation of what could or should be—she just was. There it was: a day after accepting this Church and this faith as my own, I started to understand that I was also her own. Even though she wasn't exactly like me, knowing there was room in our Church for cultural representation let me know that there was a place for me.

It was the first time I realized that I could inhabit a space as me and fully me. If Our Mother could see fit to make herself known to Juan Diego as he was, then I could expect the Church to meet me where I am in my Blackness and make room for me.

The thing is, though there have been pockets of time and spaces where that is definitely true, it isn't always. Over the next few years, I learned that even in the Church, people are people and I would still have the same struggles. In being fully Catholic and fully Black, I made others uncomfortable, and they sought to change what they didn't understand. In forging relationships, they plopped themselves on my bed like they belonged. And for a long time I tried to pay no mind to their street clothes; finally feeling as if I fit in, I didn't tell them that they were crossing a boundary that made me feel unsafe, unseen, and/or unheeded.

Over time I learned where to step to avoid the land mines so that I could stay temporarily comfortable, until one day I decided to stop. Have you met me? I am made to be seen! There isn't a bushel around that can hide my light. I learned the land mines weren't fatal and just started walking knowing I would still be unseen, unheeded, and that my vulnerability won't always be safe. There is a peace that comes with knowing there is nothing *I* can do about that.

A few years ago I had the opportunity to take the boys I worked with to an Our Lady of Guadalupe Mass in Spanish. One of my boys, who is Mexican, was feeling homesick and counting down the days until Christmas break, and I asked if he wanted to go to Mass with me that night. I printed guides for everyone to follow along, and I enticed some of my other boys with the prospect of earning extra school credit for participating in the Mass because it was in Spanish.

I loaded up my boys in the van, and we made our way to the next town over. We sang, we prayed, we took roses, and we all left the parish with renewed hope. It was on the way home that I reminded myself that the Church had room for me and that it would make room for me as I am. In celebrating Our Lady of Guadalupe, I began to celebrate myself a bit more and required others to do the same. Not celebrating in the sense of "throw me a party and tell me that I am pretty every day of the week" (though that wouldn't be so bad), but celebrating what I bring to the table instead of just tolerating me enough not to kick my chair.

Our Lady of Guadalupe, like the G she is, has my back, reminds me of my place, and keeps my bed clean. Mostly.

Imitating Our Lady

No matter our cultural background, we can all learn lessons from Our Lady of Guadalupe. Like OLG the G, we can all be people who create something new out of tension, defeat, and fear. By embracing all of the cultures present in the Church, we become stronger as the Body of Christ. Firmly rooted in our identity in Jesus, we can speak to the marginalized, the oppressed, the poor, the lonely, the hurting, and the lost in their own languages, symbols, and experiences so they know that God is a God who draws near to them.

One important way we do this as Black Catholic women is through facilitating the process of inculturation in our churches. This is not unique to our gender or culture, either—every person in every culture can facilitate inculturation. But our particular experience as Black Catholic women has taught us how others can do the same in their own lives.

As the Second Vatican Council stated in Gaudium et Spes, "The ability to express Christ's message in its own way is developed in each nation, and at the same time there is fostered a living exchange between the Church and the diverse cultures of people . . . it is the task of the entire People of God . . . to hear, distinguish and interpret the many voices of our age, and to judge them in the light of the divine word, so that revealed truth can always be more deeply penetrated, better understood and set forth to greater advantage" (44).

Women are the keepers and preservers of culture. Mothers, aunts, and grandmothers teach children the stories, symbols, and traditions of their families. Women are, more often than not, the ones who sing the songs, make the food, and repeat the proverbs in the home. In the same way, aren't we the ones who can bring our cultures fully to bear in our worship, prayer, and teaching of our faith?

We have so much to offer by bringing our particular ways of praying, teaching, and creating. Our traditions have so much to add to the understanding of who God is and how we can be better disciples. We, upon whom God has poured out the Holy Spirit, have the gifts and abilities to reveal more fully the mystery of God in our own place and time, just as *Gaudium et Spes* exhorts us. We can make space for all cultures in our parishes and advocate to bring many cultural expressions to our prayer, worship, and ministries at the same time we celebrate our own.

Our Lady of Guadalupe preserved culture. Our Lady of Guadalupe affirmed culture. Our Lady of Guadalupe formed culture. We can do all of these things, too.

After all, is she not our mother?

||||||||||||||||||||||||||||||||||||||||||||||||||||||||||||||||||||||||||||||||||||||||||||||||||||||||||||||||||||||||||||||||||||||||||||||||||||||||||||

A GUADALUPIAN COMPANION
MARTIN DE PORRES

St. Martin de Porres was born in 1579 in Lima, Peru, to a free black mother and a Spanish father. Because of the boy's dark skin and African features, Martin's father refused to acknowledge his son until Martin was eight years old. His father eventually abandoned the family after the birth of Martin's sister, leaving them to a life of poverty.

At twelve years old, Martin was apprenticed to a barber-surgeon, where he learned medical techniques in addition to caring for hair—typical of the profession at the time. After a few years, he applied to the Dominican order as a lay helper, feeling that he was not worthy to be a fully professed religious brother, in spite of his deep humility and charity. His Dominican brothers finally persuaded him to profess final vows nine years later.

Martin was well-known as a healer, both through his medical care and through miraculous cures. He was also known for his devotion to people of every race and socioeconomic level, caring for newly arrived enslaved Africans, fundraising marriage dowries for impoverished young women, and founding an orphanage. His compassion was grounded in his prayer, which was often so ecstatic that he experienced miraculous occurrences such as bilocation, levitation, and unexplained knowledge. He acted as a spiritual director to many Dominicans and was good friends with St. Rose of Lima.

St. Martin is our companion on the Feast of Our Lady of Guadalupe because, like Our Lady, Martin acted as a witness to the beauty of blended cultures and God's love of people of color. Martin's life left him every reason to despair and reject God's love, but instead he chose to love God, to love others, and to bring others closer to Christ. His radical nearness to the poor, to people of color, and to Christ reminds us of the Virgin of Guadalupe, who chose to come as one like the Aztec people, embracing their culture and drawing them closer to Christ.

St. Martin de Porres, pray for us.

REFLECTION **QUESTIONS**

1. Why is Our Lady of Guadalupe a good example of how to bring different cultures together in the Church?

2. Marcia and Shannon describe times they made the mistake of cultural appropriation instead of cultural appreciation. What do you think the difference is?

3. Shannon relates her experience of acclimatizing to a new culture and integrating many cultures together. Has there been a time when you had to adjust to a major change and integrate it into your life? How did you go about doing so?

4. Marcia talks about how Our Lady of Guadalupe helped her find a place for herself and her culture within the Church. Describe a time when you felt welcomed and affirmed as part of God's Church.

5. What are some concrete ways that you can encourage the *inculturation* of the Gospel in your home? Parish? Wider community?

3

CHITLINS, THE TEMPS, AND FAT LUTHER
Keeping Christmas

"Put on the Temps!" someone yells from the kitchen as they fix their plate. As the opening lyrics of "Silent Night" play, the mood rises and everyone sings along while piling their plates with food: "In my mind, I want you to be free . . ." Yes, that is how "Silent Night" starts. Welcome to Christmas, everyone. And it is blackity-black.

Dennis Edwards's melodic voice (backed by the rest of The Temptations, including Otis) delivers our annual sermon against the backdrop of the doorbell announcing new arrivals and the cacophony of questions about the food: "Who make the macaroni and cheese?" and "Did your mama make the dressin'?" and "Who cleaned these chitterlings? I don't eat everybody's chitterlings!" That latter is usually met with knowing looks, vocalizations of assent, and/or confirmation that they are safe.

Chitterlings, pronounced "chitlins" and referred to as such moving forward, are pig guts (well, the large intestine of a hog) and a common soul-food side dish. And yes, that sounds quite disgusting. Why in the world would we eat pig guts? Tradition. Yes, really.

The history of this dish goes all the way back to medieval England, when it was considered a peasant meal as this part of the animal was cheap in cost and quality. In the time of American slavery, slave owners knew that they had to provide food of some kind to the enslaved people in order to preserve their workforce, so they passed along the scraps that included pig ears, pig feet, and the intestines. Out of context, this does not sound appetizing.

Scratch that, it is all-out not appetizing!

We imagine that as the food was deposited in the quarters of our ancestors, it was meant to demean them. To remind them of their worth in the eyes of their masters. And to give them just enough, denying them abundance. Our ancestors, surveying the scraps laid at their feet, did not have time to despair. They didn't have the time or space to lament their offerings; instead they got to work, providing sustenance for their families and neighbors. This doesn't just apply to chitlins; this applies to most if not all of the dishes we refer to as *soul food*.

A BLACK HISTORY PRIMER
THE ORIGINS OF SOUL FOOD

What most people now call soul food originated in the cuisine of enslaved people on plantations in the Deep South, primarily Mississippi, Alabama, and Georgia. While Black Americans have developed regional foods in every part of the country (for example, the rich history of Black food in Maryland and Louisiana), soul food was carried by Black families to every state during the Great Migration[1] and became a staple of Black communities all over the country.

Soul food is a hybrid of African cuisine and foods traditionally associated with the diet of the enslaved peoples living on plantations in the antebellum South. At that time slaves fed themselves and their families on meager rations of food with low nutritional value: some kind of grain, legumes, scraps and leftover portions of meat (like chitlins), and whatever vegetables they could forage or grow in tiny gardens (most often collard greens). They also incorporated crops such as rice and okra, which were indigenous to Africa and brought on slave boats. Using local spices and herbs, along with traditional cooking techniques such as the boiling of greens, a new culinary tradition emerged.

Soul food, and indeed most Black American cuisine, developed from using what was left over and what was available to provide sustenance. It is truly American food, developed by people creating their own new culture from what they knew and what they could get, eventually moving from a cuisine characterized by scarcity to one of abundance and comfort. Like many other aspects of Black culture, soul food epitomizes how the genius of Black Americans can make sustenance even from scraps.

Soul food was born out of necessity. It speaks to not only the culinary tradition of Black folks, but also to the trauma associated with a supposed unconquerable and enduring spirit. So as plates are piled high and grow heavy with tradition and triumph, we remember our ancestors and are connected to them. As our cousins extol the taste of the greens and declare that our auntie "put her foot in them," we make promises to nurture, maintain, and sometimes improve upon the lessons that our ancestors have taught us so that we may preserve our connection to them and later our descendants' connection to us.

Soul food isn't the only thing that makes Christmas blackity-black. Like any other holiday spent with Black folks, there's the camaraderie, the checking in, the basketball game in the background, the praise of the hero who brought aluminum foil, and the start-up of the debate of Fat Luther vs. Skinny Luther (see also Big Luther vs. Slim Luther). Everyone believes this to be a dead debate topic until someone pipes up unprovoked, "You know, I think I like Skinny Luther better sometimes." Even though the music is not on a record, you can almost hear the vinyl scratch, forks drop, and grunts of dissent as the host says, "Get outta my house!"

Well, not really, but almost. This is the part of the evening when everyone has to (once again) understand here and now that Fat Luther is the superior Luther.

"Luther" (any body type) refers to R & B singer Luther Vandross, who had a successful solo career that ended only with his death in 2005. Known for his velvety voice and the songs you fell in love to, Luther (pronounced "Loutha") was a favorite in just about every Black household and part of the soundtrack of almost every Black mama's kitchen . . . along with gospel music. All of the women loved him, and when they couldn't marry him, they started their marriages to his songs and guests had a hard time not singing along as brides made their way down the aisle.

It should be understood that calling Luther Vandross "fat," "skinny," "big," or "slim" is meant to describe and not disparage. Luther's weight never factored into the love the world had for him, and hopefully that is evidenced in the fact that the authors of this book are firmly on Team Fat Luther . . . though Marcia has previously expressed that one of her favorite Christmas songs is a Skinny Luther classic—but don't tell. She doesn't think the power of love will keep her from any side-eye at the next holiday meal.

The debate about the better Luther isn't really a debate at all; it is an excuse for us to reiterate how much we loved Luther as he was, relive his greatest hits and that moment on *227*, share the joy he brought us, and affirm that he was family. We will always remember his talent, his smile, and his poise. The "debate" continues not because we don't remember who the better Luther was—we just don't want others to forget. If soul food is a tactile tradition, then soul music like the Temptations and the debate over Fat Luther are a part of our oral tradition, and they both make an impact on how we keep and share every year, every Christmas.

Amid the joy that is Christmas, there is remembrance of the past and hope for the future, despite the weariness of how far we have yet to go. The expectation is that you come hungry and as you are, so we can all eat our soul food, sing along to "Silent Night," have our petty arguments, and enjoy the moment.

One of the beautiful things about Christmas is the way it is both a universal holy day for all Christians and a unique celebration within every culture, region, and family. We are all celebrating the miracle of God's Incarnation, but we bring our individual traditions to the festivities. The multitudinous ways of keeping Christmas speak to the truth of the Incarnation. God became a human being to bring about universal salvation and peace among all nations. The Messiah came to put an end to division and to bring everyone into the fold of God's people.

Keeping Christmas, then, is more than just the food and the fun. It is also about building peace in our homes and communities and with the Lord. As people who know and love Jesus, we should be reaching out to include people during Christmas, to adapt to them, and to welcome them into a joyful community—whether in our homes or in our churches. Like the angels and the star of Bethlehem, we should be a beacon to those near and far, drawing them to join in our elation at finding God where we least expected him: lying in a feeding trough, surrounded by shepherds and kings, beginning the reign of God as an infant rather than a conqueror. If we pay attention to the meaning conveyed in our traditions, we can find God there, dwelling in our midst.

Marcia's Story

Nannie makes the best chitlins in our family. I only know this because that is what I have been told. I won't ever have the opportunity to learn for myself—I'm allergic to pork.

At first this wasn't a big deal. As I was growing up, we didn't eat pork because my mom didn't. Then one day I had some at a friend's house and learned that I was allergic. From then on, everyone in my extended family was really careful about the way things were cooked. If they knew I was coming, substitutions were made: smoked turkey instead of ham hocks, vegetable shortening instead of the traditional lard. We got beef bacon from the butcher, and we bought the name-brand gelatin. In the end, making these substitutions was better for everyone. Not only did it mean we were all included, but my family got into the habit of making soul food differently and, as it turns out, healthier.

While my family was quick to adjust, the rest of the world wasn't quite ready. Food allergies weren't catered to in the '80s like they are now, so I had to be careful and always question how things were cooked. When I was a kid, adults thought I was just a picky eater and would take the bacon off my plate, and I would spend the next day sick. In my teen and college years, I worried about being a nuisance among friends, so I would agree to doing half pepperoni or sausage on a pizza, only to spend the next day sick in bed.

As an adult, I have shown up at events where I couldn't eat much and have left hungry. First dates were awkward; every man I shared a meal with would sit across the table from me wide-eyed from my quick tutorial about my EpiPen, which I always gave even before the waiter took our drink order. It was super awkward having some of them watch me eat every bite to make sure I stayed alive. (Now I simply agree to coffee when someone wants to get to know me better.)

For a long time, the only places I felt comfortable eating were my own house and those of my family members. The world made me feel high maintenance, and home made me feel provided for and included. And that's what we expect from home: consideration, accommodation, and provision. By extension, we should get that from our Church. Instead, I am made to feel as if I need to make accommodations if I am to be considered, and the meager provisions have seen me leaving hungry.

Most of our brothers and sisters on the margins are coming to the Church hungry and as they are, but face barriers to being fed—whether it be lack of accommodation (some parishes still don't have a gluten-free host option—the equivalent of telling a vegetarian that they can "just have salad, right?"); gatekeeping (by explicitly stating there is a "best way" to be Catholic that has more to do with aesthetics than *agape*); or a lack of welcome (not acknowledging visitors, not offering worship materials in other languages). We are Catholic, which means we are a Christmas people, and we should work to bring peace and inclusion to communities that seek the same promise that we do. We should find ways to adapt to the needs of our brothers and sisters so that they will always leave home well fed.

Shannon's Story

About a year ago, my parents found an old Christmas video they recorded when I was around five or six years old. It was a tape of my brother, my sister, and me decorating the tree at our house, opening presents on Christmas morning, and finally, sitting with my dad's family to open presents. As we watched the video, we laughed with our own children about the silly stories told around the holidays and some of our favorite traditions. It was nostalgia at its finest.

In the midst of watching the home movies, though, I found my attention arrested by hearing my paternal grandmother, Margaret, speak. My eyes unexpectedly began to well up with tears because it was the first time I could remember hearing her voice since she had passed away twenty years earlier. It brought back a veritable flood of memories—watching her cook Christmas dinner with my dad and his siblings in the kitchen of her brick bungalow on the south side of Chicago; climbing up into her lap as a child to be kissed and caressed; seeing her walk proudly through the door of our parish church wearing her best hat on the day of my first Communion.

The memories were particularly poignant because we had just lost my maternal grandmother, Mary Jane, not more than a year earlier. MJ, as she was lovingly known, was a mother of ten and grandmother of thirty who loved to play pranks, sing songs around the piano, and give you clothing that was nowhere near the correct size for your age. She played tennis and golfed twice a week until she was ninety-three years old and was audacious enough to wear pants in the 1950s so she could toss baseballs for batting practice with my mom, aunts, and uncles in the backyard. She had very little time for whining children (which is infinitely understandable for a mother of ten). And, like the good German she was, Grandma loved everyone with genuine affection but kept hugging to a functional minimum (she also had forty-some hugs to give, so you can see why she kept things moving!).

I'm sure that neither of my grandmothers expected their children to marry someone from a different ethnic background. It was uncommon when I was a child to see another interracial family. Even if they had no particular objections, it was unusual. They were also different women with different interests, upbringings, and cultures.

But game always recognizes game. Both Mary Jane and Margaret were kind, generous, holy women who loved Jesus and loved their families. As I grew older, I began to see that, despite their differences in culture and personality, they had a mutual respect and admiration that helped our family embrace both cultures and traditions and participate fully in family life on both sides. They each knew that the other was good, kind, and holy—and in the end that is all that ever matters.

Christmas was a time when that difference and that unity were easily identifiable. We usually spent Christmas Eve with my dad's family and Christmas Day with my mom's side. We listened to Bing Crosby at MJ's house and the Temptations at Margaret's. Dinner at Mary Jane's consisted of turkey, ham, corn, take-and-bake rolls, gravy, mashed potatoes (obviously . . . we're Irish), and what we like to call pretzel jello.[2] Dinner at Margaret's house had everything made from scratch, including a hand-glazed ham, baked mac and cheese, sweet potatoes with marshmallows on top, and, of course, chitlins. We never felt that one was better than the other. We all made accommodations for one another so everyone could celebrate the joy of the Incarnation.

And we also brought the things we loved across cultures, too. Dad brought the baked mac and cheese and sweet potatoes with marshmallows to MJ's house, and pretzel jello began to appear at Margaret's. And no one ever made anyone eat chitlins unless they really wanted to.

While balancing two cultures wasn't always easy or simple, it was a gift. It enriched everyone because it allowed us to bring the best of who we are to the table and to share it with others. Making accommodations for the other helps us learn, grow, and find new ways of being in community. It's a way for game to recognize game and give a nod of appreciation. When we all celebrate together, everyone benefits.

Keeping Christmas All the Year

In the great Charles Dickens novel *A Christmas Carol*, it is said of Scrooge that after his conversion he knew how to keep Christmas well. If the same can be said of us, it is because of the three lessons we've outlined in this chapter: make accommodations so everyone can be included; goodness, kindness, and holiness are all that truly matter; and every culture enriches our life together (also, Fat Luther is the better Luther).

We can apply these lessons to the way we live throughout the year and especially to our life at church. For example, how many of our parishes are accessible and accommodating to those with disabilities? And we don't mean just having a wheelchair ramp into the church itself. Do we have options for those who are hearing-impaired or deaf to understand what is happening at Mass? Do we welcome families who bring their relatives with cognitive differences? How does your parish accommodate and even anticipate the needs of the differently abled in faith-formation opportunities? Do we make space for people who may struggle with mental illness, so they can enter without judgment? There are myriad ways we can be better at accommodating those with different needs.

We also need to examine how the Church can be more sensitive to the experiences of people of color. It must be more than offering Mass and religious education in a specific language. It has to be about recognizing the needs that exist in these communities and creating spaces in our parishes to address these needs. It is not enough to recognize that people of color have experiences related to their race. We must also tend to the hearts of the people in our pews on whom those experiences have an effect.

The same can be said for those who do not fit into a particular socioeconomic status. Do we expect a certain level of income for our parish programs? When people don't tithe, do we reach out to them or simply move them off the parish rolls? Have we seen the poor only as those to be given our aid or as children of God to invite into the life of Christ along with us?

We make accommodations because everyone deserves to fully participate in the life of the Church without any preconditions before they walk in the door. We make accommodations because, at the end of the day, everyone can be good, kind, and holy, and that is all that matters. When we value one way of being over another, when we value one culture over another, when we appropriate another culture instead of appreciating and celebrating it for what it is, we prevent ourselves from seeing the goodness, kindness, and holiness in others. God wants all people to know and love him. Creating environments where people can be included breaks down the barriers to knowing and loving God.

Keeping Christmas all year is about building peace by reaching out to include people, to adapt to them, and to welcome them into a joyful community. Jesus, the Word Made Flesh and Prince of Peace, was constantly reaching out, including, and welcoming others. He saw past leprosy, labels, and lies into the heart, recognizing that every person is capable of goodness, kindness, and holiness. He came to overcome the divisions between God and humanity and between humans. Breaking down barriers and working toward inclusion are at the heart of the Incarnation. Doing that hard work every day of the year is the way to truly honor Christmas all year long.

A CHRISTMAS COMPANION
BL. AUGUSTINE THEVARPARAMBIL KUNJACHAN

Bl. Augustine Thevarparambil Kunjachan lived his life striving to emulate the humility of the Incarnation and the spirit of inclusion we find in the season of Christmas. A Syro-Malabar Catholic priest, born in 1891 in the Kerala region of India, Kunjachan was sent home early in his priesthood to recover from a serious illness. During this time, he began to notice the dire circumstances of the Dalits (also known as the "untouchables") within Indian society.

Like most people of his caste, Kunjachan had ignored the Dalits because of cultural norms. They were seen as unclean by both Catholic and non-Catholic Indians and were treated only slightly better than slave labor by the majority of their society. Kunjachan began to visit the Dalits in his parish, sharing meals with them and learning about their lives. His presence in their homes affirmed their dignity and value in a way that was rare among those in different castes.

For the next fifty years, Augustine spent his life in quiet service to the Dalits in spite of the criticism he received from others. He worked to educate their children, who were not allowed in public schools; he advocated to ensure fair wages for Dalit women; and he used his own money to benefit their community. Like the God who became human as a helpless baby, Augustine entered into the lives of the marginalized and overlooked to speak to them of the love and mercy of God. At the time of his death, he had helped bring more than five thousand Dalits into the Catholic Church and to Christ.

Augustine Thevarparambil Kunjachan understood what it meant to reach out to others as Jesus did—to include and welcome them into relationship, breaking down barriers and divisions to affirm the inalienable dignity of each person who is beloved by Love Incarnate.

REFLECTION **QUESTIONS**

1. What family or cultural traditions do you have at Christmastime? What do they teach you about the meaning of Christmas?

2. Marcia talks about the importance of making accommodations so that everyone can participate in celebrating Christmas. What are some ways you can apply that idea to your home? Your parish? Your community?

3. Shannon speaks about the mutual respect her grandmothers had for each other in spite of their differences. How can you cultivate respect for people in your life who have different opinions, personalities, or cultural norms?

4. What are some barriers that you see to inclusion in your town or your parish? How can we start to remove those barriers for people to be welcomed into our communities?

4

WASH DAY

The Baptism of the Lord

"Hold still," the older woman says with stern impatience.

"I don't want to get water in my eyes!" The young girl replies as she holds the washcloth tight around her face. She squirms while standing on the chair, back bent over the kitchen sink, as the older woman diligently rinses her woolen, curly tresses until all the suds make their way down the drain.

"All done!" her mother says triumphantly, but the girl knows better. There is more. There's always more. She sits down on the chair as her mother's nimble hands unscrew the jar of deep conditioner. She stays silent and still as her mother works in the sweet sulfuric potion, "fit for a queen," that promises to make her hair silkier. Smoother. Manageable.

When her mother expertly ties a grocery-store bag over the work in progress, the little girl shimmies out of her seat and yells to her little sister: "Your turn!" She settles down to read a book while she waits. Today is wash day. And getting their hair clean is only the beginning. Soon, it will be about drying it, combing it, oiling it, and styling it. It's a twice-monthly Saturday afternoon -into-evening ritual in the young girl's house, her cousin's house, and in the homes of most of her friends.

Coif care is its own branch of Black "hairstory." It is not communicated through words, but with action and intention. Back in the day, there weren't hair-care classes for Black girls—you either had the knack or you didn't, but you knew the basics. The women in the family would make sure of that. And it starts with wash day.

Wash day is the most sacred and basic tradition of Black womanhood. Black girls are told that a woman's hair is her glory and tending to it offers reprieve and a reset.

It is a cycle in Black womanhood: you get your hair washed, you learn to wash your own, and then you wash the next head of hair that needs care and assistance. Marcia learned this as she bent over the kitchen sink in her younger years, took charge of her own hair care in early adulthood, and watched her mother shield her grandmother's eyes as she rinsed every sud from her graying hair.

A BLACK HISTORY PRIMER
BLACK HAIR

Until recently, a Black woman knew that to find hair-care products she had to go to one of two places: the section labeled "ethnic" in the hair-care aisle of a grocery or convenience store or the beauty-supply store, a one-stop specialty shop that is a staple in most Black neighborhoods. This necessity communicates to Black women, Black girls, and people in general that Black hair is different. Black hair is difficult.

Before there was a way to change it, Black women's hair was viewed as a burden. In the time of their enslavement, Black women's hair was called "wool" and deemed unseemly; their "dreadful locks" were shorn in anger and impatience, their heads covered in cloth, and their bodies treated with worse indignities.

Lighter-skinned enslaved women with straight hair had a higher asking price than their darker, kinky-haired counterparts, inadvertently introducing color consciousness that persists today. When slavery ended, Black women who styled their hair like white women were seen as more acceptable or capable as evidenced by their "good" hair.

Black women with "good" hair and/or lighter skin tones were more likely to have better jobs, education, and opportunities. As a way to even the playing field, women started using harsh chemicals such as lye and metal hot combs to straighten their hair. This evolved into wearing wigs and weaves to cover their natural hair.

In the 1960s and '70s, Black women began to reclaim their natural hair, but that didn't stick as office jobs became more attainable and Black natural hair and protective styles were seen as unprofessional in most settings. This ideology continued until a second-wave reclamation in the early years of the twenty-first century. Now natural hair is more common in every setting, and products are readily available to care for Black women's hair in its natural state.

Cleaning. Caring. Washing. Community. What do these things bring to mind for you? Could it possibly be . . . baptism? Let's talk about that for a moment.

Just as we all put time and effort into tending to our hair, we also need to take the time to lovingly tend to the graces given to us at our baptism. Whether we are baptized as infants, adults, or somewhere in between, this sacrament is the beginning of our Christian journey. Every one of us receives freedom from sin and the indwelling of the Holy Spirit at that moment. Yet, if we do nothing to cultivate that precious gift, to grow in virtue and in our relationship with the Trinity, then we'll begin to see the tangles of sin sneak back into our lives or the loss of luster that leads to apathy in our faith. Just as wash day is a reset, we need moments in our spiritual lives to return to the meaning and gift of our baptism. Intentionality is key to living a sacramental life.

Each of us is called at baptism to a great love. We accept that love in our baptism and then continue to respond to it by tending to our relationship with God through prayer, study, Christian service, and the sacraments. By taking the time to care for our relationship with the Lord, we keep our faith—like our hair—luscious, shiny, and bounteous.

Marcia's Story

My sisters and I couldn't wait for Friday night.

We had been waiting for my younger sister Joey to be old enough and then we would do it as a family, and now it was time. The date had been set. And on Friday night we were going to be official: the McGees were getting baptized.

I woke up that Friday morning, got ready for school, made sure my baptism clothes were packed, and headed out the door. When I saw Nora, I shared my news: "I'm getting baptized tonight at church!" She was confused.

"You're not already baptized?" she questioned. "I thought you were Christian." Turning to our classmate, she said, "Marcia's not even baptized and she told me she was Christian." It seems that in addition to failing to shake my implied paganism, I was now a liar. Great.

Unwilling to let my annoyingly persistent, supposed paganism deter me, I glided through my day, and when my mom came to pick us up, we made our way to our church, where we were to be baptized after service. Misha, who did not like to get her face wet, kept asking how long she would have to be under water, and Joey was asking if someone was going to hold on to her, while I was more than ready to dive in . . . and then tell Nora all about it.

My family and I stood in a line while people prayed and sang. Our pastor read a scripture while two deacons made their way to the pool. It was time. It was my lucky day; I was going to be baptized at Faith Tabernacle #1 Apostolic Church, and I would officially belong here! My mom went first. She was back up in an instant, and she really did look new. She looked relieved and more at peace than I had seen her in a long time. I was next, and my nervous excitement accompanied me to the pool. I waited, focused on breathing for a bit as the pastor prayed, then held it when I heard her say, "My sister, I baptize you in the name of Jesus Christ for the forgiveness of your sins, and you shall receive the gift of the Holy Ghost."

I felt my body hit the water, heard my heartbeat, saw slate blue waves surround me, and then it was over. The deacons helped me out of the pool, and my mother wrapped me in a towel before she went to do the same for my sisters.

On the way home, Misha piped up from the back seat, "Did you guys see the water too?"

In September 2020 I was recalling the events of that night to Shannon via Zoom when we were recording an episode of our podcast about baptism. Since I was the only one of the two of us to remember our baptism, it made sense. I usually love telling that story of belonging, peace, and unity, but this time it was strained and I was trying to hold back tears.

Earlier in the recording Shannon gave a brief explanation about baptism and, as always, I was the surrogate audience. As I was nodding along, she said something like, "All baptisms in the Catholic Church have to be Trinitarian, meaning they should be in the name of the Father, the Son, and the Holy Spirit. If someone wants to come into the Church and they haven't been baptized in that way, they are rebaptized."

She kept talking while I suddenly felt winded, confused, and stressed out. *What did she say?* I thought to myself, *I was baptized in Jesus's name and that was OK, right? No one said anything about baptism TWENTY YEARS AGO when I joined the Church! I mean, it's in the Bible. Acts 2:38, Peter said it. I grew up Protestant. All the things are IN THE BIBLE!* I regained some of my composure and asked, "All valid Catholic baptisms have to be in the name of the Father, and the Son, and the Holy Spirit?"

"Right," she answered.

"OK," I continued, "I know some of our Protestant brothers and sisters are baptized in the name of Jesus before they come to the Church." I'm sure if I go back to that episode of our podcast, I will hear the distress in my voice.

"Yes," she affirmed, then continued, "when they come into the Church, they will need to get baptized again."

"I was baptized in Jesus's name," I said, and stared into my camera meaningfully. I was looking at Shannon on the screen the moment it clicked.

Then there was silence.

Followed by the tears.

Twenty years. Earlier that month I had told someone that I had officially been part of the Church more than half my life. And suddenly I wasn't a part of the Church at all, and my baptism story felt different.

When I joined the Church in April 2000, I felt as if I left a lot behind and that I gave up a lot to make my faith my own. But I had carried my baptism with me. It was special. It was something I shared with my mom and my sisters; it reminded me of a time of my life when I learned that life was not always kind, but God was always good, and it was a bridge between the foundation of my faith and what it had grown to be. I was so sad to lose that.

In my sadness, I knew that I needed to be rebaptized. I had four godchildren (and I was the only Catholic godparent for my godson), and I was twice a Confirmation sponsor. My baptism and baptismal promises connected me to others in indelible ways.

Despite my knowing all of this, the days that followed were filled with the thought that maybe I should reconsider. As heartbroken as I was to find that I wasn't "actually" a part of the Church, I had found myself even more heartbroken from the action and inaction of the People of God. My twenty years of being "Catholic" were not without strife. I had experienced racism, sexism, indifference, and assault from those with valid baptisms. I had witnessed injustices done to my brothers and sisters on the margins with me by those who seemed to disregard their own baptismal promises, and I had felt the need to answer for the sex abuse scandal more than I should have. Maybe it was just time to leave. Maybe this was my out.

The following Sunday, I was the assigned cantor at Mass. I showed up, got my music ready, and had a word with our priest. I explained to him what I had learned and that I would not be receiving Communion, and we went on with business as (somewhat) usual. But as I held back tears during the Liturgy of the Eucharist and later while singing the Communion hymn, I realized I didn't want to leave. Jesus is here. Yes, he is everywhere, but never more present than he is in the Eucharist. As I watched everyone else receive, I felt they were also leaving me behind. I knew in that moment that if I wasn't Catholic, I wouldn't be a practicing Christian. That I couldn't go the rest of my life without a Jesus I couldn't touch.

So I chose the Church again.

I chose Shannon, the mother of my youngest godchild, and her husband Eric to be my godparents, and I chose Susan, the mother of my oldest godchild, to be my new Confirmation sponsor—creating a circle of faith, friendship, and accountability to our baptisms and baptismal promises.

Shannon's Story

My father's hair fascinated me as a child. He used to sit on the floor while we watched cartoons and let us kids comb his hair with a pick, which I did as often as I could. I loved smelling the coconut oil from his shampoo and sticking the pick in his head, where—instead of sliding off like it would on my thin hair (inherited from my mother's Irish family)—it would sit straight up in the soft, tight, kinky curls that he and my siblings shared.

As I grew up, I often longed to have natural hair like my dad and my siblings because of its interesting texture and their ability to wear it in all sorts of different ways. It seemed as if my curls would only sit a certain way and there were very few styles I could try. My DNA was different, and I felt like I was missing out on something better.

When I was about twenty years old, my sister told me something offhandedly that flipped my perspective on my own hair. She told me that she had always wished she could have my "white lady hair" when she was younger because it was so much "easier" to maintain and style. I started chuckling as I explained to her I had thought the exact opposite about my own hair. Both of us were wishing to walk in the other's shoes. It certainly drove home the platitude that the grass is always greener on the other side of the fence!

As an adult, I have grown to love my hair and find ways to experiment with what I have, rather than wishing for something I don't. I've dyed it purple; chopped it to a pixie cut; grown it past my shoulders; and arranged it by myself for formal events. It's a beautiful part of myself that I cherish for being exactly what it is.

In some ways my long road to love my hair mirrors my journey with accepting my vocation as a woman in the Church. Because our Church ordains men and not women, I know that certain roles are not open to me. As someone who works in parish ministry, who has a desire to share the Good News of Jesus Christ by preaching and teaching, I have been frustrated by the limits I must obey to do that work.

Yet as I have reflected on the gifts I bring to the Church, I have come to realize that there are so many things that I offer as a married, lay woman that no priest, religious brother, or religious sister can offer. My experience as a working parent gives me insight that a single person cannot have. My perspective as a minority woman of color in the American Church helps me advocate for those on the margins and outside of the prevailing culture. Even my pregnancy loss and my struggles in my marriage allow me to walk with others in ways that simply would not be possible for an ordained man.

God called me to this work because he wanted me for exactly who I am. My gifts and talents are my own, and—just as I can love my hair for what it is—I love my life for exactly what it is. I don't need someone else's gifts to serve God. God chose me as an infant at my baptism—Shannon, created in the divine image and called to holiness in all my uniqueness. God wants what I bring. He doesn't want to turn me into someone else.

So that's what he will get . . . with some purple hair dye occasionally thrown into the mix.

Tips for Spiritual "Curl Care"

If we were writing a tutorial on hair care, this would be the part where we would give you all of our favorite products and practical tips. So, we suppose that this is the best place to talk about how we nurture the grace we are given in baptism so we can live up to our baptismal calling to be holy and to share the Good News with others. We recommend four steps of spiritual "curl care" to honor our baptism.

The first and most important step is to spend regular time in prayer. We all know this is essential to our spiritual life. It's the first advice we offer for anyone trying to walk with Jesus. But, just as the two of us have different regimens for our different types of hair, we each have to find the "products" that work for us in our prayer life. Some people love the Rosary; some enjoy meditation. Others may journal, and still others might be best with informal prayer. While we should all learn to pray in many different ways, our faith life isn't going to have that healthy glow if we're trying to force ourselves into a mode of prayer that is uncomfortable or causes problems in our relationship with Jesus rather than drawing us closer to him.

The second tried-and-true tip we have to offer is to learn about our faith. Learning what treatment works for our hair can take time, patience, and research. We should not expect our faith to be any different. Our baptism doesn't impart all divine wisdom into our brains and hearts forever. It removes the barriers between us and God, but it creates a blank slate, not a finished product. To truly understand who God is in our lives and how to be in relationship with him, we have both devoted time to reading scripture and learning Church tradition.

How we do that is different for each of us. Shannon reads theology books and writes academic papers for fun. Marcia thinks Shannon is a little crazy. But we both do the "research" of knowing the basics of our faith and—most importantly—spending time with the Word of God.

Tip number three is to frequent the sacraments. Obviously Confession and Eucharist are essential to our spiritual lives. We also think it's important to join the community of believers for as many of the other sacraments as possible. If Confession and Eucharist are the shampoo and co-wash for our soul, then praying with those receiving the other sacraments is the leave-in conditioner that adds extra sheen and renews the texture of our hair. Our faith is strengthened and renewed when we see others commit themselves to a life of holiness in the Sacraments of Initiation and Vocation. It teaches us something new about God and encourages us to stay tethered to the Lord each day.

The final way to make sure our spiritual locks are fully luminescent is to practice Christian service. This includes small acts of kindness among our family, friends, and neighbors; acts of charity, especially the works of mercy; working for justice and equity in our local communities, nation, and around the globe; and defending the dignity of human life and promoting its flourishing at all stages, whether in the womb, in the midst of life, or on the deathbed.

Committing to this kind of intentional, meaningful care not only transforms us but begins to impact everyone around us. As we grow in love for the Lord, as we nourish our spiritual lives, we allow the living water with which Christ filled us in baptism to become "a spring of water welling up to eternal life" (Jn 4:14). That welling up, in turn, acts like a spiritual moisturizer for the "locks" of others' souls. By cultivating our own holiness and virtue we bring holiness and virtue into our relationships. When we focus on loving God in humility and joyfully serving others out of love, it concretely impacts our home life, our friendships, our parishes, our towns, even the larger world.

Take the time to discover your best care routine. Have patience in figuring out how you best tend to your heart. Love what you have been given and who you are—God certainly does! And, most importantly, rejoice in the luscious, shiny, bounteous goodness of loving God and basking in God's love in return.

A BAPTISM COMPANION
THE WOMAN AT THE WELL

The woman at the well should be every baptized person's hero. She went from skeptical inquirer to successful evangelist in the course of one day. We should all want to be that good at being disciples of Jesus.

Even though the Samaritan woman was ostracized by her community, she never gave up seeking God. We see this in her reaction when she encounters Jesus and he defies all of her cultural expectations. In response to his questions, she exhibits an unexpected curiosity and striking intelligence—challenging his motivation in discarding established behaviors between a Samaritan woman and a Jewish man; asking him for answers to the most pressing religious question between Jews and Samaritans about where to worship; and correctly ascertaining the connection between what Jesus is saying and the promise of the Messiah. For her earnestness, she is rewarded with knowledge that few others possess—that Jesus himself is the Messiah.

And the woman's encounter with Jesus allows the living water he promises to well up within her, so much so that it overflows. She is so enlightened by this encounter that she finds nothing more urgent than telling everyone she knows about him. Going to people from whom she would not expect a warm welcome, she tells them everything about Jesus and invites them to meet him, forgetting her water jug in her haste to share the Good News. Her story is so convincing that the rest of the town goes out to meet him and is changed too.

Everyone who is baptized should want to be like the Samaritan woman. We should all be so open to God's voice that we find nothing more urgent than doing his will. We should all want to be so convincing in telling our story of God's love and goodness that others come to meet him for themselves. What could be better than hearing the words inspired by her witness come from the mouths of our friends?

"We no longer believe because of your word; for we have heard for ourselves, and we know that this is truly the savior of the world" (Jn 4:42).

REFLECTION **QUESTIONS**

1. Hair care is a particularly important way of handing on tradition in Black culture. What are some memories you have of your family handing on a cultural tradition in your house?

2. Why do you think Christians need to work to cultivate the graces of baptism?

3. Marcia shares how she had to choose the Church again. Has there been a time in your life when you had to make a decision of that magnitude? Have you ever had a moment when you questioned whether you would leave the Church?

4. Shannon discusses learning to love and accept who she is, especially in regard to her vocation in the Church. Has there been a moment in your life that helped you better understand God's plan for you?

5. How can you incorporate Marcia and Shannon's four steps of spiritual "curl care" (prayer, learning, sacraments, and Christian service) into your daily life?

5

THAT CATHOLIC SHINE
Finding God in Ordinary Time

Back in 2016 the world was introduced to the phrase "Black Girl Magic," a term used to describe that which is particularly phenomenal about Black women, celebrating our uniqueness, beauty, and excellence in every facet of our lives.

Black Girl Magic is not simply a hashtag to affirm our inherent goodness, but also a way to prompt Black women to bring their own "magic" to the world. When we share our Black Girl Magic, we bring the best of our culture to others—our food, our fashion, our history, our literature, our music, our art—all the best of our cultural inheritance. We also bring our individual greatness—our intelligence, grit, persistence, gentleness, hope, humor—all the gifts of being humans created in the image and likeness of God. By loving our Blackness, loving ourselves, and looking for ways to share those gifts with the world, we allow our Black Girl Magic to alight on everything around us and make it shine, too.

We like to think that there is a corresponding awesomeness in our faith that comes from the grace we receive at baptism, and we call it "Catholic Shine."

Catholic Shine, at its heart, is a way in which we walk through the world looking for signs of God's presence and finding beauty in the mundane that reveals the mystery of God in all its resplendence. It is a worldview that sees everything as a sacrament—that is, a visible sign of God's grace, which makes that grace present and effective in the world. All of creation is imbued with something indescribably phenomenal, full of beauty, wonder, and uniqueness. By keeping our eyes open to the small moments of grace in the everyday and sharing with others about those moments when God touches our lives, each of us brings our Catholic Shine to the world, becoming a sacrament of God's grace in our own right.

While each liturgical season helps us better understand and reveal the mystery of God, Ordinary Time is a particularly important season for cultivating our Catholic Shine.[1] The other seasons focus on specific, essential moments of the mystery of salvation, and rightly so. Ordinary Time, on the other hand, takes up the majority of the year and—though it has its own celebrations and feasts—lets us find a steady rhythm of discipleship to mark the weeks, months, and years of our life with quiet, consistent faithfulness in whatever walk of life we find ourselves. It is the time when we must find joy, peace, patience, hope, trust, and mercy in the everyday stuff of life. It is the time when we need that Catholic Shine the most and when it can best reflect the divine radiance found in every corner of the world God has made.

Marcia's Story

In January 2020 I was in a slump. I had just turned forty (which was not without fanfare, thank you very much!) and was coming off one of the worst years of my life. I had lost a lot in 2019 (a good friend to cancer, my uterus, and my respect for the writers of a certain prestige premium-cable fantasy drama with dragons and thrones, to name a few), and this new year didn't start that well either, so I didn't have much hope. One Sunday I found that I had a case of the mundanes . . . meaning that I was feeling unremarkable and generally not great.

I woke up exhausted, which is never a good sign, and made my way to the bathroom, where I caught a glimpse of myself in the mirror.

You guys, if it could have cracked, it would have cracked. And I'm not saying that to be funny, I truly believe it!

"Well, God," I said, looking at my reflection, "this is the face that you love." I splashed some water on my face and went to make coffee.

For over twenty years, I've been reminding God that my face at its most hideous is still one that he loves. Red, puffy eyes? God loves that face. Drool? Wrinkles? Crow's feet? Ashy as the day is long? All loved. Sometimes it is that reminder that gives me the boost I need to pull myself out of a slump or a rager or a pity party.

"The face that God loves" is not a phrase I created. A friend of mine sat me down once and read me a passage from the book he was reading at the time. In an attempt to help me through a bad spell, he shared some insight into how worthy of love I was. Now is probably a good time to tell you that the incredibly confident woman who wrote the words you are reading right now has only been around the last decade or so. She used to have extremely low self-esteem and a raging eating disorder, so the idea that God loved anything about her was laughable.

I'm so glad that I am not that girl anymore, but the fact that I can be her again at any moment is enough to keep me focused on who I am and whose I am. And that's what I needed that January morning. So I reminded God that he loved my hot mess of a face and made my coffee. For good measure, I took a selfie with my coffee mug and posted it on my Instagram stories, where it would live for the next twenty-four hours to be scrutinized by the masses. And it didn't bother me . . . I figured that if anyone had a problem with it, they could take it up with God— it was one of his faves, after all.

I did the same thing again the next day, and the day after that, and so on because it felt good not to be curated on social media. It felt nice to take a picture of me with sleep in my eye and looking like I needed every bit of coffee in the mug I was holding. I was embracing the mundane with abandon, and I was taking all of my followers along for the ride.

About a week later I added "#MugShot" to all of my morning selfies, and I made sure to feature a different mug every day (I collect a wide variety of mugs). This had been going on for about two months and I didn't think anyone was paying attention to my morning ritual, until one clumsy morning when I managed to break seven (SEVEN!) of my mugs in one fell swoop. I posted about it in my stories that morning in the hope that someone would be sad with me.

The next day someone messaged me and asked for my address. She said she was sad about what happened to my mugs and wanted to send me a new one. She told me that it makes her day to see me posing with my coffee every morning. I couldn't believe it! My mundane morning ritual was bringing someone else joy.

Over the next year, other people embraced their vulnerable moments and started posting their own mugshots and tagging me in their mundane morning selfies. #MugShotNation was born. We are a community of people who celebrate the unremarkable moment before their first sip of coffee, and it is so beautiful.

Extra ordinary wouldn't be possible if we didn't embrace the ordinary. Most of life's moments happen in the mundane, and that's where the miracles are born. Not every moment is going to be the best moment ever, but every moment is great. I am not particularly cute before coffee, but God uses that face that he loves to remind other women of who they are and whose they are. Embrace the mundane because there are miracles waiting in the wings.

Shannon's Story

The only advice I ever give any couple embarking on marriage comes in two parts: "Try not to have two babies in one year. But if you have to, make sure it's the same insurance year, so the second baby is free."

As can be inferred from my advice, I did have two babies in one year and the second baby was, in fact, free.

In addition to two infants, we also had a four-year-old at home at the time. Eric had been offered a new, higher-paying job that required our family to relocate, and after the move I took a part-time position so that I could be home with our kids for the majority of the week. Even though it was an adjustment after years of teaching, coaching, and youth ministry, I enjoyed having the freedom and flexibility to spend time with my little ones, especially during the early years.

As much as I loved being with my young children, however, there were times I felt as if I wasn't accomplishing anything. I felt that I had much more to offer the world, especially the Church, than cleaning bathrooms, folding laundry (my least favorite thing in the world), and changing diapers. I wanted to pursue a graduate degree. I missed the positive impact I knew I had in full-time ministry. I worried that by removing myself from professional circles, there would no longer be a voice for people of color when decisions were being made at my parish. And, in my most selfish moments, I envied the advancements Eric was making in his career while I sat at home. I couldn't understand how the daily routine brought much glory to God.

One September I was able to take a much-needed retreat, thanks to the generosity of my mother-in-law, who stayed in our home to watch the kids. Since my route took me right past his graduate school, I scheduled lunch with my friend Mike, who had shared my office in my very first parish youth-ministry job more than a decade earlier. We caught up as we talked about the usual joys and trials of married life with small children, swapping war stories of life in ministry, too. But it was an offhand comment that he made that stuck with me when I drove away that afternoon to my retreat.

"You're doing the works of mercy," he said, "taking care of kids. You're clothing the naked, and feeding the hungry, and it's hard work."

Mike's remark was a moment of Catholic Shine that helped me uncover a spiritual truth for my life. Childcare was draining. But it was also a sacrament.

Childcare was the way I was living out my discipleship at the moment. It was a way for me to make the love of God present for my children and my husband. It was a way for me to encounter God in their love. Divine beauty was peeking through the stacks of dishes. Divine light was glimmering like the stars above me during the midnight feedings. What I was doing was revealing the hidden mystery of God's glory because, when I was loving others, Love Incarnate was there with me.

The realization didn't change the way I felt about laundry (I would gladly pay someone to sort, fold, and put it away). But it did help me put things into perspective. What my family needed of me at that moment was to serve them, and in doing so I was serving God. In that season, I brought my Catholic Shine to the world as a wife and mother first, with everything else coming second. Now, as my children get older and my life at home changes, my Catholic Shine can light up other places. It does not make what I do now more holy or more important for the kingdom of God. It's simply a new way of using my gifts and talents to bring God glory.

I am a better person and a better disciple because of the time I spent at home. Those years were the years I began working as a diversity educator and interfaith minister. That was also when I began my master's degree. I helped my students start a Black student union and Black History Month celebrations; I also wrote an entire curriculum to study the Bhagavad Gita with Hindu teenagers. I joined my parish choir, went to retreats at a nearby convent, and acted as an alumni mentor for a theology student at my alma mater. It was a time full of grace even if it was a time of staying home.

Life isn't one set of exciting adventures after another, just as the liturgical season can't always be Christmas or Easter. Sometimes discipleship is about finding God in the first sip of coffee and laughter at a friend's corny joke. God's grace fills the moments in between the highs and the lows. God's grace permeates Ordinary Time.

Shine Your Light

Every baptized person has that Catholic Shine. Each of us is, quite literally, God's gift to the world, revealing the divine presence in the midst of the everyday. We are all "little s" sacraments—visible signs of the invisible reality of the divine, making God's grace present and effective in our world.

Part of the gift of Ordinary Time is finding our own way of bringing the Catholic Shine of a sacramental worldview to those around us, of being sacramental signs in our homes, parishes, and communities. It is a season to contemplate the teachings of Christ in order to apply them to our own place and time as his disciples. By looking for God's presence in our individual daily experiences, we are better able to identify the movement of the Holy Spirit around us. Through this introspection we can identify the ways that we as individuals best understand God and, hopefully, determine how to bring our gifts and talents to our particular state in life.

The intersection of God's work in our lives and our unique giftedness is where our Catholic Shine shines brightest. Think of those people who radiate God's love in your own life or the saints whose holiness is most relatable and inviting. They make God's grace present because they embrace exactly who they are and love others as they come. Living with that Catholic Shine doesn't change anything about what the world is. Rather, it allows us to see beyond the veil to the divine imprint that has always been present and pulls back the veil for others to see it, too.

So, go out there and get that healthy glow. Spend some time basking in God's radiant light. Get yourself a spiritual suntan. And then show off that Catholic Shine for the world to see.

AN (EXTRA) ORDINARY COMPANION
ST. FRANCES OF ROME

When looking for a saint to help us find God in the ordinary, we can't think of anyone better than St. Frances of Rome.

Frances was born in 1384, the daughter of a wealthy nobleman and his devout wife. Though Frances wished to enter the convent, her father arranged her marriage to a young nobleman named Lorenzo de' Ponziani, much to her chagrin. After they married, Frances disliked the parties and hosting duties that were expected of a woman of her station and clashed with her mother-in-law over it. Frances soon found an ally in her sister-in-law, who also wished to devote her life to prayer and service of the poor. With the support of their husbands, the two spent time in prayer and acts of charity, while also attending to their duties at home and taking care of the children who came with the passing years.

Only three years after Frances married, her mother-in-law passed away, leaving Frances to run the household at age sixteen. She did so while continuing her charity, eventually winning over both her husband and her father-in-law to her way of life. Lorenzo even permitted her to establish a lay order of women under the Benedictines called the Oblates of Mary. Lorenzo died when Frances was fifty-two, and she moved into the Oblate house to live as their superior until her death four years later.

Frances is a saint who demonstrates that holiness can be lived in every season of one's life. She brought her Catholic Shine to the poor in the streets of Rome as well as to the homes of the rich and powerful. She discovered that the desires God put into her heart to serve him were not meant to be lived only one way; by being faithful and listening to the voice of the Holy Spirit in her everyday life, she could take the ordinary and make it extraordinary.

One of Frances's most famous sayings speaks to the wisdom of finding mystery in the mundane. "It is most laudable in a married woman to be devout," she said, "but she must never forget that she is a housewife. And sometimes she must leave God at the altar to find him in her housekeeping."

St. Frances of Rome proves that extraordinary lives are possible by imitating Jesus in whatever walk of life we inhabit. Our lives are no less sacred or impactful simply because they are ordinary.

———

REFLECTION **QUESTIONS**

1. What do you think it means to have "Catholic Shine" that brings mystery to the mundane?

2. Have you had moments when, like Marcia, you realized that you needed to appreciate what was good about everyday life rather than trying to find the perfect moment? How do you keep that perspective in the day-to-day?

3. Was there a time in your life when you felt, like Shannon, that your day-to-day was insignificant? What helped you find purpose in that period? Where did you see God's grace present?

4. What do you think it means to say we are "little s" sacraments? How can our lives make God's grace present in the world around us?

6

REFINER'S FIRE
Lent at the Foot of the Cross

Asking God to purify our hearts is dangerous. Yet it is exactly what the Church does in Lent. Scripture provides a myriad of references to the love of God acting as a refining fire to purify even the hardest of hearts. When precious metals are thrust into the refiner's fire, they are placed at the hot center of the flame in order to burn away any minerals that would reduce their sheen or prevent them from being shaped and molded. Asking God to purify the heart means being prepared to endure the blaze.

As a Church we step into the fire in Lent, beginning forty days in which we may endure painful purification in order to come out transformed. Our commitment to the practices of deeper prayer, increased fasting, and more generous almsgiving will not always be pleasant or easy. But if we do them well, we may be as tested and fine as the purest gold and silver.

The refiner's fire of Lent is the way of the Cross. Taking the first step on the Via Dolorosa is stepping into the fire. We must be willing to pass through the conflagration of the Crucifixion in order to reach the Resurrection. We must walk our way to the foot of the Cross and remain there for a while, as the fires singe away the rough edges of our hearts.

The fires that refine our faith are not always of our choosing. Black Americans, whose legacy of faith has been forged in the furnace of slavery, have struggled with the tension between pride in our culture and resentment at the unnecessary and horrific evil that led to its creation. When the two of us reflect on the meaning of Lent in our own lives, we experience the tension of choosing to enter into refining fire and at the same time grappling with a fire that we never chose. In Lent we sit at the foot of the Cross, companions of the Crucified One, pondering the incomprehensible paradox of the ultimate good coming from the greatest of evils.

We invite you to join us as we take our first step into the flame.

Shannon's Story

Anyone who knows me knows I hate Lent. The austerity and deprivation of the season have a way of making me slightly depressed and more than a little cranky. Every year when Ash Wednesday rolls around, I grumble and gripe about how I wish we could skip Lent and go straight to Easter.

I can blame my Lenten malaise on a few things. However, if I'm being honest with myself, I will admit that I dislike Lent because it makes me confront the uncomfortable truth of the Cross.

Lent is a reminder of the blood and shouts and horror at the foot of the Cross. Like the cold hand of Dickens's Ghost of Christmas Future, Lent points unwaveringly to the grave, and I do not want to acknowledge the inevitability of death. Lent asks me to confront my own rejection of God, my own mortality, and the fact that we live in a world still mired in the muck of sin and death. Lent is also a reminder of the times when I felt I was the one being nailed to the Cross instead of Jesus: losing a child to miscarriage; losing former students and family members to suicide; even struggling with depression, anxiety, and suicidal thoughts while pregnant.

To confront the Cross is to confront the worst of my life and the worst of human nature. It's not something I look forward to.

My unwillingness to enter into Lent is paralleled by my reluctance to confront the legacy of slavery in my own history. Even though no one on my mother's side ever participated in human trafficking in the antebellum South, I wrestle with what it means to be both the descendant of slaves and the descendant of white people who, even if unintentionally, benefited from the color of their skin when they came to this country. It's also terribly painful to imagine the torture that my Black ancestors endured during the Middle Passage, as well as lynchings, beatings, and the realities of plantation life. I would prefer to move on and live my life in the present because there are no words to express the pain and trauma of slavery.

When I was nineteen years old, there came a day when that avoidance was no longer possible. As a sophomore at the University of Notre Dame, I had just been accepted into a peer education group at the counseling center. It was the early days of the internet, and our biographies and photos that were added to the department's website to highlight the program were available to the public through everyone's favorite search engines. That was also the year I was studying in Italy, and I was writing regular updates for the international program's website on my experiences studying abroad.

One day I received an email through my school account from a man in Texas who shared my last name and was doing some genealogical research. Since my maiden name, Wimp, is rather uncommon in the US, most people who share it are related in some degree. He was trying to find other branches of his family and wanted to know where I traced my family tree.

In the Black community in Chicago, our family, though small, was fairly well-known. My grandfather served as the supply officer for the Tuskegee Airmen in World War II. My great-aunt Kay sang in Duke Ellington's band. On the whole, we knew all the members of the different branches of our family tree.

The man who contacted me was not part of any of these branches because he was white. For a Black American who is descended from slaves, having distant white relatives usually means one thing: their family members owned the plantation where our family members were enslaved.

A BLACK HISTORY PRIMER
AFRICAN AMERICAN GENEALOGY

For African Americans, tracing family history is a complicated endeavor. As mentioned in the introduction, it was common practice during the slave trade to obfuscate family records and countries of origin, as well as to separate families to maximize profit from human trafficking. For this reason, most Black Americans researching their ancestry have trouble tracing their families beyond the 1850s, past the generation that was alive at the end of the Civil War.

When that generation began its life after enslavement, most did not have last names passed down from their family. Because they needed to adopt a legal last name to be considered citizens, many chose their own. Some honored American history by adopting names such as Washington or Jefferson. Many simply took on the last name of the family that owned the plantation where they had lived all of their lives.

The legacy of slavery is also one of the reasons Black Americans have strong fictive kinship networks, or the inclusion of those who are not biologically related or related through marriage into the extended family network because of a strong bond of friendship and trust. Because biological and marriage ties were not always a guarantee of familial bond (especially when one's biological family may have also been the owners of the plantation where one was enslaved), Black men and women created kinship networks with those around them to build communities of care and support that extended families often provide.

So there I was, confronted by the reality that a man descended from our family's "masters" was reaching out to trace our family ties and—because of my very Irish name and light skin—likely had no idea that I was African American. I did not know if he was aware that there were Black members in the family tree, nor how he would respond when I told him. It was a very real intrusion of the legacy of slavery in my life—a moment in which I had to decide if I was willing to open the door to the hurt, pain, and anger of my family history or keep it locked away in a corner of my mind to be allowed out only when it could do me no harm.

I remember walking down to our dorm chapel, making sure it was empty, and then uttering all of the expletives I knew in front of the tabernacle in order to express my confusion and resentment toward God for this situation. I realized that acknowledging a family connection would mean pursuing peace instead of anger, reconciliation instead of self-preservation, and trust instead of control. It meant doing, in a small way, what Jesus did in the Garden of Gethsemane: making the choice to walk the path to Calvary in the hope that it would lead to an empty tomb.

The next day, after all my ire with God had been expressed (if not totally spent), I decided to reply to the email. Taking my heart in my hands, I wrote about my family, whom I loved dearly and was so proud to call my own, hoping in spite of myself that my first attempt to heal my own wounds would not open them up even more.

When I received a reply the very next day, I was surprised. The man said he was already aware of my grandfather through military records and asked to be put in touch with my dad. Over the next few months, the two would talk semiregularly, as the man was very interested in learning more about the Black members of the family. He even provided information about the names and places of residence of some of our ancestors that we had had trouble tracking down.

There was no cinematic moment in which anyone begged for absolution for the sins of slavery. There was no inspired speech about coming together as one family. There was no grand gesture of forgiveness by our family to theirs. And I still had to work through my grief and indignation about why, even though I love living in America, my Black family actually ended up here in the first place.

None of this was beautiful. It was the ugliness of crucifixion. But it was also the first step in paving a way forward for myself and for my family.

My family cannot change what happened to us. I cannot change why I am here or how the legacy of slavery has impacted my life. But I can choose to follow the example of Christ. I can choose not to run away from the suffering and the hurt, but instead to be vulnerable to the possibility of being wounded and broken. I can trust God to strengthen my resolve when I would prefer to be spared the pain, to help me to do the things I need to do to establish equity and justice in our country. In my community, my home, and my personal life, I can take action that upholds the dignity of all people—even the family of the former slave masters whom I might be tempted to believe do not deserve it.

I know I cannot ignore slavery just as I cannot ignore the Cross. Like every American, I must approach that horrifying sin with courage to tell the truth of what it was. Only then can we begin to see how we might overcome the wounds that it has inflicted on our nation. As a Christian, I also know that the Cross is not the end of the story. It may be the fiery furnace through which we must pass, but it refines us into the finest gold. Slavery is part of my legacy. It is the ugliness of crucifixion. But there is glory to come if I am willing to keep taking the next step.

Marcia's Story

As I was growing up, my church started every new year with a for-ty-day fast. From January 2 until February 10, we denied ourselves food from sunup to sundown, committed to prayer, affirmed our community, and renewed our trust in the Lord. Schoolchildren were not expected (or permitted) to participate on weekdays when school was in session, so my sisters and I joined my mom in fasting on the weekends. We went to church with her every single night (that means twice on Sundays), and every year we would join my mom in prayer for a specific intention.

Some years we didn't have a car, and we had to take public transit to evening service from the north side of Chicago all the way to the south side of the city, in the dead of winter. And we did it without complaint. Well, at least not loud enough for my mom to hear. She always reminded us that we were making a sacrifice over the course of forty days, not only for a reward on earth, but for one in heaven as well. Since heavenly rewards are literally out of this world, my sisters and I kept our grumbling to a minimum as we stood on cold L train platforms waiting for the fifty-five minute reprieve the ride would give us before making the trek home.

Struggle is no stranger to me. It's no friend, either.

Looking back, I can see that the sacrifice my mom accepted and volunteered us for did bear fruit. My sisters and I don't hesitate to go to God in prayer, we show up for him in times of feast and famine, and we all own cars. Before it was a Pinterest quote with #BossBabe, my mom taught us that growth happens outside of our comfort zone. With or without intent, she made us comfortable with discomfort. I inherited my complicated relationship with struggle from my mother, and she inherited hers from my grandmother.

For better or worse, struggle is synonymous with the Black experience and especially Black womanhood, as more is expected and demanded and significantly less is given in return.

I was taught to work hard, and excellence was always the expectation. I should point out that while this came with some pressure, I always felt loved when meeting expectations proved to be a challenge. My family's standards were not about ego; they were always communicated because my thriving depended upon it, though I didn't learn why until I was twelve years old. That was the year I started seventh grade, and it was the first time I was the only Black kid in the room.

After my first day of school, riding home on the 22 Clark bus with my mom, I told her about how I had struggled to understand an assignment in class and would have to ask the teacher for help. My mom turned to me and said, "Make sure you do." And that day, my mom gave me the "twice as good to get half as much" talk as we made our way home.

"Twice as good to get half as much" is the mantra successful Black people and those reaching for success say to themselves. I previously thought those words belonged to my family—that they were a part of McGee family folklore that scared all the grand-kids into academic submission. Yes, submission. Because of the value put on a good education and the success that could stem from one, future survival hinged on the ability to submit to and meet the academic standards of the moment. I remember hav-ing a meltdown between classes in high school, thinking I was going to be on food stamps all of my life because I didn't have the best grades, didn't get the lead in the musical, and didn't win a student-government election. While I recognize these sorts of pressures are anxiety inducing for other teens regardless of race, as a Black girl I wasn't thinking about how I might fail to provide for my future family; I was always faced with the reality of how I had to get to a place to provide for my current one. Being twice as good to get half as much wasn't just about me—if I got more, I could reach back and give more.

Upon learning that I wasn't the only one who carried the bur-den of being the hardest-working, least-rewarded person in the room, I felt a little less alone. "Twice as good to get half as much" carried me from middle school into high school, college, early adulthood, and my forties. Those words are still true thirty years after I first heard them. The struggle, as they say, is real.

If you're reading this and think the math doesn't add up, you're right. It doesn't. And so it goes where injustice is involved. The truth in this mantra silently touches every aspect of life, and I remain conscious of its impact.

When I was in school, I had to raise my hand more, read ahead more, volunteer more. In professional settings I had to produce more, smile more, know more. When making new friends, I had to contribute more, show more excitement, and compliment more. When I did just as much as my white classmates, coworkers, and friends, I watched others get the recognition, raises, and relationships, and I got to fall behind even though I was falling in line. Looking back, I realize that I would wonder if "twice as good to get half as much" applied to our faith life and standing with God. I observed that my white classmates went to church a whole lot less (an hour on Sunday, that's it!), if at all, and they didn't have to wait on cold L train platforms to get there. It wasn't until I was in college that the suspicion fell away.

This societal unconscious bias that breeds the expectation of Black people having to do twice as much work has, I believe, roots in a time when we did not count as a whole person.

A BLACK HISTORY PRIMER
THE THREE-FIFTHS COMPROMISE

In the early days of the United States of America, the delegates to the 1787 Constitutional Convention reached a compromise on how to count enslaved people when determining a state's population. This was an important question because the method of calculation would affect taxes and the apportioning of state representatives.

The three-fifths ratio was originally proposed as an amendment to the Articles of Confederation in 1783. It was intended to create a shift from real estate to population as the basis for determining each state's wealth and tax obligations. The Southern states objected to the formula because it included slaves when calculating taxes even though they were primarily viewed as property.

According to the compromise, three-fifths of the slave population of an area would be counted for purposes of taxation and representation, whereas the total number of free Blacks would be counted. The US Constitution states the following: "Representatives and direct Taxes shall be apportioned among the several States which may be included within this Union, according to their respective Numbers, which shall be determined by adding to the whole Number of free Persons, including those bound to Service for a Term of Years, and excluding Indians not taxed, *three-fifths of all other Persons.*"

So while enslaved people were denied voting rights and full personhood, and were still regarded as property, there was debate as to what extent they should be counted as people of the land—ignoring, of course, the matter of their human dignity.

|||||||||||||||||||||||||||||||||||||||||||||||||||||||||||||||||||||||||||||||||||||||||||||||||||||||||||||||||||||||||||||||||||||||||||||||||||||||||||||||||||

Making my way in the world and making an impact are only possible if I can prove that I am five-fifths of a person. How do I do that? I have to be twice as good to get only half as much. And I can't stop working if I want the other half. Whether I am struggling to make a grade or earn a promotion—I long ago stopped trying to make friends with those insistent that I work for it. I am on a journey for a worldly wholeness along with other Black people who hope to thrive in this world.

"Twice as good to get half as much" has seeped into my life in the Church.[1] When I accepted a position in a multiparish ministry setting and was rebuilding the program, I was regaled with stories about how the previous youth minister fell short while parents and teens expressed their needs. The "last minister" wasn't present, they said. She handed off responsibilities to parent volunteers, and parish secretaries said they never saw her. There weren't enough fellowship activities, opportunities for participation outside of the Sunday night meetings, or mission trips.

The previous minister, for whose deeds I was to atone, had been there for five years and only left because her husband's job demanded their relocation. Otherwise, it appeared, I wouldn't have gotten the job.

Feeling the expectations were high and the bar was long, I hit the ground running. I assessed what I had to work with, figured out what I needed . . . and by the end of my first year I was exhausted. I was working six days a week trying to be equally present at three parishes (no matter the difference in resources), initiating fellowship activities three days a week, attending school events, doing lunch-break check-ins, and offering service opportunities (including two mission trips). By my second year, I had added two more mission trips to the program offerings. My third year, I expanded the Confirmation program, so I asked for more volunteers and community support to make it happen.

And suddenly, one of the pastors was constantly checking behind me and asking me about how I was spending my time. It was exhausting and confusing; I felt the strain in my relationships in every parish. Even though I was working well over sixty hours a week (all the while making sure I was present, available, and enthusiastic), the message was that I wasn't doing enough.

After a meeting with the pastors, I was told that my contract would not be renewed for a fourth year. I felt that I had met and exceeded expectations, had amazing relationships with my teens and their families, and thought I formed a great community.

Before I left, one pastor, Fr. Steve, told me that he appreciated all of my work but that, in the end, another pastor, Fr. Bill, no longer wanted me as coordinator. Fr. Bill wanted to take the youth ministry program in a different direction, and I wasn't part of the vision.

Hurt and confused, I gracefully ushered in my replacement and coordinated all the end-of-year activities. In the back of my mind I really felt my race played a part, but there was no way to know for sure. I left my job and my church community feeling hurt, deflated, but not completely defeated.

Six years and two jobs later, one of the parish secretaries reached out to me on social media to set the record straight. To paraphrase, she (the former parish secretary) had been fielding calls from angry parents during my third year. They didn't like my new Confirmation program, and they didn't like me. She told me that I was being called lazy and inefficient, and the pastoral team decided that instead of talking to me about it, the solution was to monitor me closely. Fr. Steve had asked her to make sure I was working all of the hours for which I was being paid. The thought was that if no one saw me working, then I wasn't (mind you, I was a youth minister and did not work the same hours as everyone else). She was asked to report any mistake I made, no matter how small. She knew it was wrong because she saw how hard I worked, and she knew it was racist because it wasn't being asked of anyone else (she had fielded a lot of complaints about other staff members during her time at the parish). It is possible she just didn't know how to question her boss and her pastor and so went along with it. And I lost my job. So there it was: I worked twice as hard as the person before me, and I received almost exactly half as much in an incredibly insulting way. I was actually only given three-fifths.

Racism. Racism is what holds me back, keeps me working harder than I should, makes me feel as if I can never do enough, and allows others to discount me. It persists in my moments of suffering, in the moments of striving for worldly wholeness, and now it was confirmed that I would have to strive for wholeness among the People of God.

The struggle, I will tell you again, is real.

That revelation of the events surrounding the loss of my job did not cause me to leave the Church, but it was hard to see God when those who served him contributed to my suffering and loss of livelihood. It would be one thing to see this as an isolated incident, but I have been Black in many Catholic spaces, and I have had to work twice as hard to be seen, heard, and included. I have had to sing louder, pray harder, and kneel faster before I am welcomed. Before I am recognized as family in my own home.

I know that in the eyes of my Father in heaven and to most of my sisters and brothers in Christ, I am whole, but there are places in the world and even in the Church where I consistently fall two-fifths short, or so it seems. I remain in the tension of balancing my worth in God's eyes (which I don't have to earn) and my worth in the eyes of his people (which I feel I will never work hard enough to earn fully).

As I hope to be understood and welcome as I am, I often feel as alone as I did on L train platforms in the January cold as a child, waiting for reprieve from this struggle until I can feel completely welcome at home.

Hope at the Foot of the Cross

As we were grappling with how to confront the legacy of slavery and racism in this book, someone asked us a very insightful question. "Knowing that the trauma is there and will always be there," she asked, "do you think there will ever be a day when it won't affect us anymore?"

And that is the real question Americans must ask of themselves. Will there ever be a day that our racial identity will not affect how we are treated and will not impact our flourishing as beloved children of God? Can we ever heal the wounds inflicted by this sin?

The answer, we believe, lies in Lent. It lies in sitting at the foot of the Cross and recognizing that suffering can never be forgotten, but it can make us better and lead us to salvation. We cannot skip over Lent to Easter, just as we cannot gloss over the truth of how Black people have been treated in our country. We must acknowledge it fully, completely, with sorrow and repentance in our hearts. We must allow the fire to refine us.

But the Cross is also our greatest hope. We, as Christians, know that God can and does bring about all that is good. We pray, hope, and fervently work for racial justice in our nation because we know God can bring it about. The wisdom of the elders teaches us that we may not see it accomplished in our own time, but every small step toward equality brings us closer to the day when it will be complete. It will be the work of generations, but it is God's work and it can be accomplished.

Refining fire is uncomfortable. Doing the work is uncomfortable. But gold can only be refined one way. We, Church, must finally allow the impurities to burn away.

A LENTEN COMPANION
VEN. AUGUSTUS TOLTON

If anyone deserved to be angry at the Church, it was Ven. Augustus Tolton. Born into slavery in Missouri and baptized Catholic as a baby, Tolton fled the plantation with his mother and siblings. They were able to escape captivity and claim their freedom in Quincy, Illinois, just over the Mississippi River, where they settled for the rest of Tolton's childhood. When his mother enrolled him in the all-white parish school, Tolton, his family, and the pastor were threatened and harassed by the other families until he was withdrawn to attend the public school. Thankfully, a priest named Fr. McGirr took Augustus under his wing, making it possible for him to attend another parish school and eventually encouraging Tolton in his vocation to the priesthood.

But again Augustus met prejudice and discouragement. No seminary in the United States would agree to educate a Black man, and it took two years and a petition to the Vatican for Tolton to finally enter the seminary in Rome. On the eve of his ordination Tolton was so discouraged by the racism he had experienced in America that he wrote to friends and family expressing his desire to be assigned to Africa.

God's plans for the saintly priest, however, would be different. Tolton was to return to Quincy after his ordination, becoming the first known Black priest to serve in America.[2] Though Fr. Tolton was extremely disappointed, he returned home in obedience with the intention to serve with hope and faithfulness.

Unfortunately, Fr. Tolton once again encountered harassment and prejudice. One particular priest in Quincy actively strove to defame Fr. Tolton and undermine his efforts in his parish. The harassment became so bad that Fr. Tolton requested, and was granted, permission to transfer to the Archdiocese of Chicago, where he served until his premature death at the age of forty-four.

In spite of the pervasive racism that Fr. Tolton experienced, including the trauma of slavery, he consistently spoke of his love for the Church, the sacraments, and the many wonderful examples he had among the priests and religious sisters who educated him. He worked to uplift the Black communities where he was assigned and spoke with joy about his vocation to the priesthood. He worked tirelessly in his parishes to share the love of God with those around him and to bring the sacraments to the people.

Fr. Tolton, who walked through many refining fires, is a perfect companion for Lent. His words, born of his trials and his joys, inspire us to keep on keepin' on, grateful for the gifts God has given us, which far outweigh the trials:

"I shall work and pull at it as long as God gives me life."

REFLECTION **QUESTIONS**

1. Why do you think Shannon and Marcia say that entering into Lent is "dangerous"? Is that a good thing?

2. While Shannon's story of confronting the legacy of slavery in her family is unique, all of us have had moments where we had to confront hard truths or endure things we wish we did not. When in your life have you had to endure pain or hardship? What sustained you in that time?

3. Marcia talks about the reality of how racism has made it so Black people need to work twice as hard to get half as much. Have there been times when a part of your identity has prevented you from being recognized for your work or achievements? How do we fight against these ideologies that prevent people, especially people of color, from truly flourishing?

4. How can Lent help each of us admit and work through the hard truths in our own spiritual lives?

5. What are some concrete ways Catholics can "step into the fire" by working to acknowledge and overcome the legacy of slavery in our country? In our Church?

7

IT LOOKS LIKE YOU'RE LEANING
Trust and the Triduum

In the classic '90s rom-com *While You Were Sleeping*, one of the most unexpected jokes comes right in the middle of a major disagreement between the two romantic leads, Lucy (played by the incomparable Sandra Bullock) and Jack (brought to life by the irresistibly charming Bill Pullman).

Jack, who is attracted to Lucy even though he believes she is engaged to his brother Peter (who happens to be in a coma and knows nothing about Lucy), accuses Lucy of infidelity to his brother with her neighbor, Joe Fusco Jr. The suggestion is laughable to Lucy and the viewer, who know that she has rejected Joe over and over again and that she is secretly in love with Jack in spite of her fake engagement to Peter. But Jack, who knows nothing about any of this, saw the two innocently hugging in the stairwell and misconstrued the scene.

When Lucy tries to explain that she was simply hugging Joe Jr., Jack argues that she was not hugging him—she was "leaning."

What, we may ask, is "leaning"?

As Jack's description implies, "leaning" involves a spark of attraction—chemistry between two people that acts like a magnet, pulling them closer together physically in their mutual desire to connect with each other. As Jack describes "leaning," we see that he and Lucy begin to exhibit the same behavior, mutually closing the distance between them until they are inches away from a possible kiss.

Suddenly, we hear the rough voice of Joe Jr. ask Lucy if Jack is bothering her because, Joe Jr. says, "It looks like he's . . . leaning."[1]

In some ways, our relationship with God can be described in the same way Jack describes "leaning." When we catch a glimpse of the goodness and glory of God, it draws us in like a magnet, pulling us closer and closer to the Lord. God, too, pursues us in love as we draw near to him, the mutual desire for love sparking deeper connection.

The fulfillment of that mutual desire finds its liturgical expression in the Triduum (Latin for "three days"). The high holy days of the Church year—Holy Thursday, Good Friday, and the Easter Vigil—are the moment when the great love story that God writes in salvation history is remembered by his Church and when we respond to that invitation into the divine life. On these three days we commemorate the great gift of the Eucharist; we stand in awe of the unsurpassed mercy of the Passion; and we open the floodgates of God's divine favor through the Sacraments of Initiation and the renewal of our baptismal promises. The Triduum teaches us to give in to the attraction and fully lean on God.

Marcia's Story

Let's take a trip to beautiful Hawaii. The year was 2005, and I was running my very first marathon, 26.2 miles. It was about two in the afternoon. I had been moving since six that morning, hit a wall hours ago at mile 17, and didn't want to move anymore. That was when I reached mile 26, and I felt as if it was finally over. I pulled out my flip phone to call my mom as my stride quickened.

"Mom!" I screamed into the phone.

"Are you OK?" she answered.

"Yes! I'm fine," I said, "I'm just about to cross the finish line, and you're coming with me!"

My mom got excited, and I could picture her in the basement of the church where I grew up, shushing people so she wouldn't miss the moment when I crossed. After a significantly uncomfortable time went by when I was just breathing heavily and coughing into the phone, she said, "How much farther, honey?"

I looked ahead and realized that I was nowhere near the finish line.

"I'll call you back," I said, snapped my phone shut, and resumed my pathetic shuffle.

I crossed the finish line about five minutes later and called my mom sometime after I jumped in the ocean to celebrate. Every marathon after that I made sure to hold off celebrating at mile 26 because that last 0.2 miles is part of the race. It is a painful, uncomfortable part that makes the race longer than I think it should be, but I can't celebrate until it's done. Each and every time I run long distance, I must learn to leave behind my expectations of what I thought this race was going to be, pace myself, and do all I can to keep going.

Even before I became Catholic, that's how I felt about Easter and the days leading up to the celebration. When you grow up Black and Protestant, Easter is all about the pageantry. And from the time you get home from school on Thursday, it is all about preparing for said pageant. First, I had to make sure I had everything I needed for my Easter dress. On Friday, my mom, sisters, and I did last-minute shopping before the Easter pageant rehearsal, where I made sure everyone knew I had my speech memorized. By early Saturday morning, my sister Misha and I were in Miss Brown's kitchen getting our hair pressed and curled (an all-day event that would result in Easter-worthy hair with minimal scarring as long as we stayed still and held our ear down when we were told). On Saturday night we set our hair in rollers, ironed our clothes, and put all appropriate accessories together so we would be ready to celebrate our risen Savior in style with every hair in place.

When I was done with classes on Holy Thursday in 1999, I was ready to make my way home for the weekend, excited that I had no expectations of making an Easter speech, pressing my hair, or buying a new dress. I was a sophomore in college, and those days of pageantry were a few years behind me. Before I headed to the train, my friend Joe invited me to Mass that night with him and his other friends who were hanging around for the weekend. We squeezed into his Thunderbird and made our way to a church a couple of towns over. We took our seats and waited for Mass to begin.

I leafed through my program and saw how involved it all was. Now, I went to Catholic school so this should have been nothing new. We always had an all-school liturgy on Holy Thursday, but this was nothing like what I signed up for or was used to! The story of Jesus's last night on earth was haunting and beautiful. I remember focusing on my breathing as I tried to keep the tears behind my eyes. This was the most beautiful church service I'd ever attended, and I suddenly felt underdressed in my denim skirt and tights. Settled in my seat at the end of the pew, I stood and kneeled in unison with everyone else, but I stayed focused on everything at the altar.

After years of being told that Jesus is present in the Eucharist, I finally believed it on April 1, 1999, and the joke was on me for not realizing it sooner.

Just a month before, I had exited that church after Mass proclaiming "Protestants rule!" (seriously, past Marcia is legit cringeworthy). Now, walking out with my friends that evening, all I wanted to do was go back. I needed to go back. I had to go back—with the same fervor as Jack Shephard in the season-three finale of *Lost*. I didn't go back that day . . . instead we went out for ice cream, and I went home for the rest of the weekend. I had expected to spend some relaxing time helping my mom with the

Easter baskets, but I felt on edge. Part of me was working to reconcile my new, deeper understanding of the Church with what I had been taught about its inferiority.

As I went to bed on Good Friday night, the finish line seemed so far away. I wanted to celebrate Easter right then, and I wanted to celebrate it with the people who had surrounded me the night before. Instead I was lying awake, breathing heavily, coughing, and shuffling along. Slowly making my way to the Church I would someday call home.

"Triduum" is a glorious word that I didn't know the first twenty years of my life. It reminds me that I am almost there. The thing about the Triduum is that you still have to pace yourself. You have to know the prize is coming, and you work to maintain your joy and hope. Lent may leave you limping or shuffling along, but the Triduum will keep you moving.

Shannon's Story

As a self-professed liturgy nerd, the Triduum is my favorite time of the year. It is the Catholic Church at its very best—rituals, music, symbols to the max. Every year I get a little giddy thinking about what is coming, like the washing of the feet, the veneration of the Cross, and the chanting of the Exsultet. From Holy Thursday to Easter Sunday, there is barely anything that can quench my delight in being Catholic.

With one exception.

A few years ago, on Good Friday, I was scrolling through Facebook (as one does when one is fasting and needs a distraction to stay out of the pantry). An article popped up on my news feed titled, "Should Praise-and-Worship Music Be Used at Mass?" and I noted that my diocesan director of youth ministry, a friend of the original poster, had commented on it saying, "Yes, this is so great!"

Now, as a liturgy nerd who wrote her master's thesis on the Mass, I was in my element. I love praise-and-worship music, but I don't think every song is appropriate for Mass. Plus I love a good argument about how to best do liturgy to bring out the meaning and the mystery of the Mass.

So I clicked. As I read, I could see that the article had a more traditional European bent, as I expected, and made a case for a return to choral music, the organ, and, where possible, the Tridentine Latin Mass. I enjoy reading these types of arguments as I think they bring an important voice to how to best represent a European cultural expression of the faith for people of European descent. But when I got about halfway through, the direction of the article changed. The author began to argue that this particular expression of the Mass (one highly influenced by the cultural milieu of post-Reformation, Enlightenment Europe) would bring "cultural enlightenment" to "uncivilized people" in places such as Africa and Asia, claiming that "even these people" recognized that this way of celebrating the Mass was "more beautiful" and culturally "superior" to other ways.

I was shocked. Did someone living in the twenty-first century actually write that Africans and Asians were uncivilized, uncultured people? So I did exactly the opposite of what I should have done . . . I waded into the comment section. There, right next to my diocesan director's comment about how good the article was, another woman commented, "Ugh, yes! My parish sang 'Were You There?' on Good Friday instead of 'O Sacred Head Surrounded.' It was terrible." My diocesan director liked that comment.

I felt sick to my stomach. A song that meant so much to me as an African American—a song born out of the crucible of slavery to express the well of despair of my people, a song that allowed us to identify with our Lord and Savior as one who suffered like us and who transformed that suffering into redemption—was being disparaged because it was not European. The holy people of Africa and Asia who bring so many of their cultural symbols to the Mass were being told they were savages who needed European culture to teach them the truth about who God was. It was exactly the opposite of what the Church teaches about inculturation.

And on top of that, the person who represented the diocese and the bishop was agreeing wholeheartedly with all of it. How could I celebrate being Catholic when the institutional Church seemed so untrustworthy? How could I lean on God when I was afraid that if I were to lean on God's people, they would let me fall? When the Body of Christ wounds me, how am I supposed to see Christ present in their midst as I celebrate the Paschal Mystery?

My anger was so hot that I almost wrote a rant in the comments (which is extremely effective and charitable, right?). Instead I took a breath and sent a message to my director explaining how I felt. We had a personal relationship, and I trusted that if I reached out to him as a friend and a devout Catholic, he would understand where I was coming from. We had a very good exchange in which he came to realize how his comments might affect other Black Catholics in the diocese and why the cultural implications of the article were more worrisome than whether or not we should use praise-and-worship music in Mass. He deleted his comments and tried to do his best to address my concerns.

The rest of that Triduum, I was relearning that God, while present in the Church, is not the Church. God is trustworthy, and we can trust him even when his people disappoint us. If there is any lesson from the Passion, Death, and Resurrection we celebrate at the Triduum, it's that God can take the worst of human failings and transform them into joy.

Leaning on the Lord

If the spiritual life can borrow Jack's explanation of "leaning" from *While You Were Sleeping*, it must also move from the give-and-take of attraction to the firm foundation of trust. It is no longer leaning in toward the Lord, but rather leaning *on* the Lord. The Triduum may be the high point of the liturgical year, but it is also a turning point. For those newly initiated, it is the beginning of their lifelong discipleship as Catholic. For those of us who have been disciples a little longer, it is the spark of Easter joy and a renewal of our commitment to share the Good News of the Resurrection with the world.

The Triduum reminds us why we trust God and encourages us to give in ever more fully to our dependence on him. We know we can trust God because of the great things he has done. We know his track record, and it is perfect. If God has done it before, we surely know God will do it again.

We can continue to lean on the Lord because God has never failed us. We have come to this point in our own faith journey because we love God and believe in his promises. Like the author of Lamentations we can proclaim,

> The LORD's acts of mercy are not exhausted,
>   his compassion is not spent;
> They are renewed each morning—
>   great is your faithfulness!
> The LORD is my portion, I tell myself,
>   therefore I will hope in him. (Lam 3:22–24)

The divine love story is still being written in our hearts as well as yours. We hope that our passion is evident and that our trust inspires hearts to trust in turn. We hope that when people see us seeking after God, it is so obvious how much we love him that they can't help but say, "Excuse me, ma'am, but it looks like you're . . . leaning."

━━

A TRIDUUM COMPANION
THOMAS THE APOSTLE

Poor Thomas. He is most known for a small bit of doubt, so much so that, when we were talking about him for this book, Marcia said something like, "I feel like I hear about Thomas the Apostle all the time . . . why don't I know much about him?" The embarrassment was palpable when she realized that he was, in fact, the doubting Thomas from the cautionary tale she'd heard in her youth.

There is so much more to him than his disbelief, so let's talk about our good friend Tom.

Thomas the Apostle loved Jesus and was so committed to the Lord's message that he was willing to follow him always. My guy, Thomas, somewhere in between ride or die and stage 5 clinger, like many (if not all) of the early disciples was often confused by Jesus's words and was one of the only ones who spoke up when he needed clarification. He was like, "Umm, Jesus . . . where are you going? Also, I want to go to there!" In his desire to be nearer to Jesus and to serve at his side, Thomas should cause us to reflect on Christ's nearness to us in all aspects of our lives. Thomas's faith should inspire us despite his doubt. Yes, he had to see to believe. We have all felt that way at some point, and to have him as an example puts us in good company.

Our good friend Tom is a great companion for the Triduum, not only because he was there for the first one, but because he is our model for taking Jesus at his word. St. Thomas trusted what Christ had to say; he followed Jesus where he went; and when faced with his teacher, he recognized his Lord and God and proclaimed it.

REFLECTION **QUESTIONS**

1. Have you experienced the magnetic pull of "leaning" toward God that Marcia and Shannon describe? How did that moment impact your faith?

2. Marcia reminds us that the Triduum teaches us how to pace ourselves in the life of faith. How can you apply the idea of pacing yourself to your own faith journey?

3. Shannon talks about a time when she felt hurt by the institutional Church and by fellow Catholics. Have there been times in your life when you were angry with the Church or other Christians? How did you respond?

4. What are some of the great things God has done in your life? How does remembering them help you trust God more fully?

8

MADE FOR SUCH A TIME
Embracing Easter

We've deliberated over the matter and unanimously agreed. Queen Esther can come to the cookout.

Now this metaphorical gathering is normally limited to Black folks. It's a get-together for the culture. But those outside the Black community can garner an invite from those inside. To get the coveted golden ticket you have to prove that you can hang; you can handle some seasoning on your food; and you are down with Black culture in all its fullness and beauty. If you can sing along to Gerald Levert and you know why you don't want to be called a jive turkey, you're pretty much guaranteed in.

Back to Esther and her invite . . .

Esther, according to the book bearing her name, is a Jewish woman living in Persia who is selected as a member of the harem of Emperor Ahasuerus (a fictional character loosely based on the Persian emperor Xerxes), eventually becoming his queen. Her husband is deeply in love with her but is unaware of her Jewish heritage.

When the king's adviser, Haman, who hates the Jews, convinces the king to put every Jewish person in the kingdom to death, Esther's uncle Mordecai—a surrogate father who raised her from a young age—begs Esther to intercede. Esther, knowing that Ahasuerus can by law put her to death for coming into his presence without being summoned, initially refuses. In response,

Mordecai writes her another letter, reminding her that her status and privilege bring responsibility.

"Do not imagine," he writes, "that you are safe in the king's palace, you alone of all the Jews. Even if you now remain silent, relief and deliverance will come to the Jews from another source; but you and your father's house will perish. Who knows—perhaps it was for a time like this that you became queen?" (Est 4:13–14). The story ends with Esther saving her people because she pleads for them before the king. Through her, a moment of fear and pain is transformed into a time of hope. Through her, God makes a way out of no way.

Esther can come to the cookout because she was willing to step out in faith and trust God. Through her agency God saved the Jews, giving them hope when all seemed lost. Esther, guided by Mordecai, was not afraid to speak truth to power and act at her particular moment in history for what she knew was right and good. And, if you've read the story, you know that she throws a great banquet—so she definitely knows her way around some seasonings.

The story of redemption when hope seems gone is, of course, the story of Easter. God takes the hurt and despair of the Crucifixion into the unimaginable joy of the Resurrection. Both the triumph of Esther and the great triumph of Jesus's Resurrection are stories of God drawing new life out of circumstances that led to a tragedy. Neither excuses nor denies what terrible pain has been inflicted, but both make something new and beautiful from the darkest moments of grief.

Easter is a celebration of our great fortune in receiving God's gift of salvation. Coming out of the penitential period of Lent, we acknowledge that, though we cannot forget the moments of darkness, we can find joy in their remembrance because of how God has transformed our wounds for his good.

We believe this is especially true of us as Black Catholic women. We live in a time when our faith and our history speak most urgently to the challenges that confront our Church and our nation. Though our people have lived through persecution, injustice, and fear, those wounds have so much to teach others because our unique culture is a transformation of those wounds into joy. Just as the wounds of Jesus remain on his resurrected body because they tell the story of God's victory over sin and death, the lived experience of Black Catholics holds power to reveal God's ability to turn every darkness into light. Like Esther, perhaps we were made for such a time as this.

Marcia's Story

"The women came with spices fair to the tomb where he was laid . . ." I muttered under my breath, practicing my Easter speech. I had a reputation to uphold—I had never frozen or forgotten my speech on Easter Sunday. Ever the performer, I was prepared. It was 1993, and I had my game face on. It was my job to tell everyone that . . . Jesus rose from the dead.

Both of my grandfathers and one of my grandmothers were preachers. The Easter speech was my sermon, and I was doing my part for the family business. Maybe.

When I was growing up, Easter was the big show and speeches were a big deal. Everyone under the age of eighteen was expected to participate in the Easter pageant in some way, and I was a triple threat: I gave a speech, sang in the choir, and filled Easter baskets (my mom was in charge of that last one and made me help her).

In addition to being my moment to shine, every year my Easter speech taught me something new. In 1994 I met my very first saint companion, though I didn't know it at the time. Now in high school, I had the better part of a chapter in the book of John to memorize and recite for my Easter speech: John 20:1–18 to be exact, and I killed it! I had voices, and inflections, a weeping Mary Magdalene, and a sympathetic angel.

"Woman," I said, channeling Nannie for my most sympathetic voice, "why are you weeping?"

And then in my most confident voice, I ended my speech proclaiming the risen Christ: "I have seen the Lord!"

I like to believe that I received thunderous applause when in reality I was probably ushered off the stage so that the next person could go on, but that speech stuck with me for a long time. I only knew Mary Magdalene from what I read in scripture, but I knew she had something our pastor called "holy boldness."

Holy boldness means having the ability to step out in faith and proclaim the risen Christ in spaces and places where others may not be comfortable. It includes working for justice in the name of Jesus. Holy boldness involves being comfortable with getting uncomfortable and inviting others into your discomfort for their edification. Holy boldness doesn't pull any punches when it comes to protecting Jesus's message or God's people.

When I converted to Catholicism, I knew whose name I would add to mine at Confirmation. Mary Magdalene had been walking with me for years. Guiding me as I spoke truth to power, comforting me when I wept, reminding me of when I have seen the Lord and, in the moments that I feel faint, that he is risen.

Mary Magdalene was the bridge between the faith my family chose for me and that which I chose for myself, and she has been there every step of the way. Holy. Bold. And beautiful.

Shannon's Story

For the rest of my life, I will likely call the summer of 2020 the Summer of Black Lives Matter. Because of the deaths of multiple unarmed Black men and women, including Ahmaud Arbery and Breonna Taylor, protests swept the country at the same time a pandemic ravaged the lives of hundreds of thousands of people. In addition, prominent Catholics all over America were busy downplaying or denying the racial injustice and inequality in our country—often justifying their opinions with harmful stereotypes and little attention to statistics or the lived reality of Black people.

As a woman of African descent who is also Catholic, I was not surprised at the backlash against the protests. The history of the Church in America and my own past experience had conditioned me to believe that when racism reared its head, the Church would remain silent and ignore the very real pain of my people.

So I did what any self-respecting millennial would do in the midst of pain, anger, and frustration: I wrote a social media post about it. In all seriousness, I was tired of the tacit refusal to address racism. I had never heard it discussed in a homily or at a Catholic conference, or written about by a major Catholic media outlet. The Catholic Church in America has—unfortunately—a long history of complicity and silence in the face of the larger structural problems that create the racial divide in America. I love the Church because the fullness of life in Christ is here and the sacraments are here. Yet, as a woman of color, I have also wondered whether my voice would ever be heard or represented in the Church I love.

In the summer of 2020, I believed that nothing would change because nothing ever had after all the previous protests. I believed the internet was the only place where my voice might be acknowledged. I certainly didn't believe it would be acknowledged in my Church.

I was surprised, upon uploading my post, how many people felt the same way—not just Black Catholics, but people of every ethnicity. They were frustrated and felt a desire for the Church to do more than simply shake its head in muted sadness. And as the weeks went on, I saw clergy, religious, laypeople, and even bishops begin to take bold, prophetic action to address the sin of racism. Media, conference organizers, and diocesan offices began to reach out to Marcia, me, and other Black Catholic speakers and writers to give workshops, host cultural competency training, write about our experiences, be keynote speakers, and advise on policy. I realized that there were, in fact, many people in the Church who truly wanted to work for justice and equity because they believed that was what God wanted. Marcia and I were even invited to become founding board members of Catholics United for Black Lives, a nonprofit organization advocating for racial justice in alignment with the teachings of the Catholic Church.

Sitting in adoration on Holy Thursday the next year, one year after the beginning of the COVID-19 pandemic and the BLM protests, I was struck by how much gratitude I felt over the changes I had seen in the Church in the past year. I was also humbled at how God, through my past experiences, gifts, and talents, had prepared me to meet that moment. Because I was obedient to the voice of God in many other moments, I found myself invited into the work of the Spirit on a much larger scale. I, like Esther, was in a position to change what lay ahead because of the opportunities God had prepared for me leading up to that moment.

That Easter I clearly saw the pattern of resurrection out of death and purpose out of pain. Though there is still much work to do, I have great hope. No, we cannot bring back those who have died or pretend our nation has overcome racial injustice. Just as the wounds of Christ are still visible in his Resurrection, our wounds have not disappeared. But like his wounds, ours can be transformed by glory. They can become instruments of our redemption, healing, and hope.

Grace Abounds All the More

At the Easter Vigil, the Church calls the first sin of Adam a "happy fault" because it has won so great a Redeemer. The irony of the statement speaks to the heart of the Easter story. Even though our sin and pain are great, the elation of the Resurrection is so much greater that we can even be thankful for the lowest moments.

God, though not the creator of sin, can work even through sin for our good and to bring about our redemption. God takes what we give him, no matter what we give him, and uses it to demonstrate his limitless love. In the deepest despair of sin, we can also find the highest heights of grace. The Easter story is that no horror that we have ever created as humans has been enough to overcome the glorious power of the risen Lord. In the words of St. Paul, "where sin increased, grace overflowed all the more, so that, as sin reigned in death, grace also might reign through justification for eternal life through Jesus Christ our Lord" (Rom 5:20–21).

Easter teaches us that joy is possible after pain and despair and that joy makes the pain bearable. The horror of the Crucifixion cannot be forgotten if we want to understand the euphoric joy of the Resurrection. The Resurrection loses its full mystery and meaning if we pass over the agony of the Cross. But Easter's power lies in the truth that we can acknowledge the hurt without forgetting it and still rejoice in the redemption made possible because of it.

As Black people, we cannot forget the many horrors, tragedies, and injustices that have befallen our people. Like wounds that have been stitched together, these past sins have left scars that cannot fully return to wholeness. But in the Black Church (in which we include both Protestants and Catholics), we find an example of how we live as Easter people, a people who move forward from the harrowing grief and ongoing trauma of racism in America to become a Church resurrected: by holding tight to the hope of the Resurrection, standing firm in community, and working for the coming of the kingdom. The Black Church was made for such a time as this.

A BLACK HISTORY PRIMER
THE BLACK CHURCH

Africana people across the world have been Christian from the time of Christ—Matthew 27:32 and Luke 23:26 mention St. Simon of Cyrene (an ancient city in Libya) and Acts 8:26–40 details St. Philip's baptism of the Ethiopian eunuch—mainly practicing their faith within the Orthodox and Catholic Churches. Black Americans, however, are predominantly Protestant and practice within the seven denominations known as "the Black Church."[1]

These denominations began because Black congregants and Black ministers were frequently excluded or denied places in white congregations of the same denomination. The racism experienced by Black Christians led them to form their own churches and mutual aid societies, such as the Free African Society of Philadelphia, founded by Richard Allen and Absalom Jones in 1787. This organization, with strong ties to the Episcopal Church, eventually gave rise to the African Methodist Episcopal tradition and other long-standing Black Episcopal congregations. These churches became anchors for the Black community, allowing for places of respite, renewal, and support, especially in promoting Black culture and advancing the cause of racial justice. It is no accident that the Civil Rights Movement of the 1950s and '60s was formed, grounded, and led by ministers and lay leaders of the Black Church.

Black Catholics, though they did not break with the Roman Catholic Church, often experienced the same discrimination in their parishes that caused their Protestant brothers and sisters to create their own worship communities. Before the abolition of slavery, many bishops, priests, and religious orders kept people enslaved—often using their unpaid labor to build Catholic institutions. Even until the twentieth century, Black Catholics were often seated in segregated sections of parish churches or denied Communion until all the white parishioners had received first. Black children were frequently prevented from attending Catholic schools, and Black parishioners were forced to build their own separate parishes and schools. While these congregations were not separated from communion with the pope and bishops, they often served the same role as the Black Protestant congregations, sustaining the faith and hope of Black Catholics for the continued pursuit of equality through the gifts of the sacraments and the support of the Body of Christ.

|||||||||||||||||||||||||||||||||||||||||||||||||||||||||||||||||||||||||||||||||||||||||||||||||||||||||||||||||||||||||||||||||||||||||||||||||||||||||||||||||||||||||||||||||||||

A Way Forward

The Black Church, in both Catholic and Protestant congregations, has always clung to the hope of the Resurrection. The liberating power of Christ's victory over sin and death has been a focus of the preaching, prayer, and worship of Black Americans since the secret gatherings of enslaved people in "hush arbors" in the antebellum period. Nowhere is this more apparent than in the hymns and spirituals we sing—songs like "Steal Away to Jesus," "Power in the Blood," "Soon and Very Soon," and "Give Me Jesus." Even the simplest of these songs speaks of hope in God's promises despite pain and heartache. They tell us of a God who keeps his word and whose peace cannot be stolen away by any principalities or powers. This hope bubbles up in joy even when it seems the powers of the world look victorious.

Every Christian should have this same hope in God's promises, the same unfailing belief that God's peace will always be a wellspring ready to overflow within us. Easter people live in the light of the Resurrection, knowing in advance who wins the final battle and how the story ends. The faith of Black Christians, refined by the fires of history, shows us that Easter joy is never extinguished. It is always present, sustaining our hope and transforming woundedness to new life.

The Black Church also teaches us that Easter people stand firm in community. Black congregations have historically been a cornerstone of the wider community, a place where social connections can be forged and spiritual needs can be met. They have been a safe haven to be among one's own, to breathe easy within one's culture, and to worship in freedom—to be our own people with no expectation to conform to another way of being. The strength of each person is bolstered by the community and restored by our shared history, culture, and faith. That is not to say every community is perfect, but rather that the church is the place where the individual and the community find mutual help in each other.

This same strength can exist in every parish. Every parish can be a place to build connections and to encounter the love of Jesus. Every parish can be a place that makes individuals feel safe and able to express their full selves. It can be a place of restoration where the wounds of life are mended and each of us can reflect on our shared history as people redeemed by a righteous and merciful God. The Black Church teaches us that our strength is in our unity and our shared bonds—not to conform, but to come as we are with all of our joys, hopes, struggles, and unique traits that enrich and fortify the whole.

For this to happen, we must leave certain things at the door: our politics, our socioeconomic status, our cultural preferences, our unchecked biases, and the barriers we put in place to our hearts. To be an Easter people, we must be willing to be vulnerable to the other and to listen to the other without predetermined notions. It is work that every single person must do, not simply the clergy and leadership.

To be an Easter people, every one of us must take responsibility to see all those who walk through the doors of the church as brothers and sisters in Christ with their own hopes, fears, dreams, and stories of redemption to be heard without judgment. We must see each individual as a gift God gives to our community to reveal more about who God is and how much he loves. A church that allows people to celebrate their personhood, their culture, and—most importantly—their election in Christ as children of God is a church that can bridge every false division between people created by the world.

Finally, the Black Church teaches us that Easter people work for the coming of God's kingdom. This means that the Church goes beyond providing spiritual balm for those within its walls; it also works to change the social, economic, and political realities around it to be more just and reflect more fully the truth of the Gospel.

The Black Church has long been a force for social change and social support for the community. Congregations and denominations have worked within their local communities and on the national level to advocate for policy changes in many organizations (think of the Montgomery bus boycotts, which were organized through local churches). They have provided economic support for their communities, too, such as collecting funds to help escaped slaves settle in Northern cities in the antebellum period and providing college scholarships to youth in Black communities today (check out all the amazing work of the Knights of Peter Claver and the Ladies Auxiliary for just one example). Black Catholics in particular have been instrumental in working in the prolife movement by establishing organizations that operate from a consistent life ethic, which honors and protects human life from conception to natural death and every stage in between.

An Easter people who cherish the hope found in Jesus and who stand firmly rooted in welcoming communities cannot help but go out into the world to share that joy with others. An Easter people sees that the love of God is not limited to any one place, but needs to permeate every part of creation. An Easter people knows that God's kingdom, while never fully complete on this earth, is breaking out among us here and now. We imitate the One who hears the cry of the poor, the One who defends the widow and the orphan, the One who welcomed prostitutes and tax collectors to his banquet table. An Easter people works for peace, justice, and the flourishing of all life. We confront all that works against peace and life, even if it is difficult or painful, because we are following in the footsteps of the Crucified One in order to share in his Resurrection. We do the work to build the kingdom of God on earth because we have been lucky enough to experience it ourselves.

Alleluia Is Our Song

The genius of the Black Church is the truth that Easter people do not shy away from addressing hard things. We do not ignore the Crucifixion. Instead, we find the triumphant joy of the Resurrection in the victories that our faithfulness to God and—more importantly—God's faithfulness to us have made possible. While we do not rejoice in the unnecessary evil, we shout, "Hallelujah!" in response to what God created in spite of it. Christ has taken the sins of racism, discrimination, apathy, and anger upon his shoulders and transformed them into beauty, peace, truth, and unity.

Easter people do not stay in the upper room hiding like the apostles did before Pentecost. They go out, preaching, teaching, healing, and serving in concrete ways. Like the apostles, they go to where people are and speak the Good News to them. They lay hands on the sick and hurting to heal them and offer forgiveness through relationship with Jesus Christ. They find the poor, the widows, the orphans, the downtrodden, those in prison, those without food, shelter, and clothing, and strive to meet their immediate needs, and also to change the systems that keep them from having access to basic human necessities. They challenge culture where it is lacking, bringing unfailing hope in the great deeds of God in Jesus Christ without fear of the powers and principalities that may oppose the flourishing of God's chosen people. They do the work to change their own hearts and rid themselves of every sin and burden that clings to them to prevent them from loving God and others without qualifications.

Easter people transform wounds into glory.

Every single baptized person has died to sin and risen with Christ. Every single baptized person shares in the Resurrection.

We are, to quote Pope St. John Paul II, "an Easter people, and 'Alleluia' is our song."[2]

We, the Catholic Church in America, are an Easter people, so let us be an Easter people! We already have everything we need. We have the fullness of life in Christ through the sacraments. We have the height and breadth and depth and width of the Church's teaching. We have the divinely inspired Word of God, the witness of the saints, the deposit of faith, and the guidance of the successors of the apostles. If we are willing to acknowledge and address the wounds that exist in our country around race; if we are willing to put in the work to begin to counteract the effects of racism; if we are willing to work for the coming of the kingdom, then we will see new life spring up all around us, and our nation and culture will be transformed by God's work among us. We are ready-made for this work. We, dear friends, were made for exactly such a time as this.

AN EASTER COMPANION
JOAN OF ARC

St. Joan of Arc exemplifies a woman who made the best of tragedy and responded to the call of God in her own time in faith, even when it required great courage.

From early in her life in Domrémy, France, where she was born in 1413, Joan was said to have experienced visions of the saints. One such appearance in her thirteenth year led her to seek out the French prince to offer herself in service to the French army in their war against the English. Through various miraculous visions and supernatural wisdom, Joan was able to help the French army to victory, preserving much of the kingdom of France. Though she often said she would prefer to stay home with her mother, she chose to act in faith to help her people, convincing generals, kings, and theologians of her piety, and riding into battle . . . all while wearing pants.

Even when she was captured, sold to the English, and put on trial, Joan maintained her humility and trust in God's will. During her trials she continued to demonstrate piety and spoke truth to power as the English tried over and over again to find evidence that she had committed heresy. Even in death, she asked for a cross to be held in her line of vision so that she could keep her eyes fixed on Christ.

Joan of Arc was made for her time. She responded to the call of God to do what was needed even though it was not what was expected or even what she herself wanted. Joan made the best of tragedy and stayed faithful to who she knew God to be. She knew that in the Cross of Christ she had found her hope and that no power was greater than the resurrected Jesus who had called her his own.

We want to be like Joan: courageous and humble, trusting and confident . . . especially if we also get to wear pants.

REFLECTION **QUESTIONS**

1. Where have you seen evidence of God drawing new life out of the circumstances of a tragedy?

2. Do you have holy boldness like Marcia? What can you do to cultivate spiritual courage in yourself?

3. How do you think we can transform the wounds of racism into healing, as Shannon says? What gifts do Catholics bring to the work of racial justice?

4. What are some of the lessons that you think the universal Church can learn from the Black Church?

5. What would it look like if our individual parishes lived as an Easter people?

6. How is the Catholic Church made especially for the time we live in? What do we have to offer the world that it can't find anywhere else?

9

MY WHOLE BLACK SELF
The Power of Pentecost

What does it mean to be Black and Catholic? It means that I come to my Church fully functioning. That doesn't frighten you, does it? I come to my Church fully functioning. I bring myself, my Black self, all that I am, all that I have, all that I hope to become, I bring my whole history, my traditions, my experience, my culture, my African American song and dance and gesture and movement and teaching and preaching and healing and responsibility as a gift to the Church.

—Servant of God Thea Bowman, Address to the US Bishops'
Conference, Washington, DC, June 1989

Homilies for Pentecost often encourage us to put ourselves in the shoes of the apostles as the Spirit came down. And that is legit. But also, imagine being in the crowd when the apostles burst forth from the room. You see people who you know can't speak a word of your native language all of a sudden shouting with joy, praising God—and you can understand them perfectly. You probably think they are crazy. And it's no surprise that the people gathered wondered if the apostles had been hitting the bottle a little too hard that day.

The wonder of the Holy Spirit is that the Spirit's gifts make something completely unbelievable possible. The fearful become courageous. The shy become bold. The hesitant become wise. When God sends the Holy Spirit, things go down.

The same Spirit of God poured out on the apostles is sealed in us in the Sacrament of Confirmation. In the sacrament, the bishop lays hands over those to be confirmed, calling down the Holy Spirit and asking the Spirit to give them the seven gifts. Then, as the bishop anoints each one with the sacred chrism and speaks the words "Be sealed with the Holy Spirit," they also receive a permanent character—that is, an indelible mark on their soul—making them witnesses to Christ. Through that seal, that character, as the *Catechism of the Catholic Church* quotes St. Thomas Aquinas in explaining, "the confirmed person receives the power to profess faith in Christ publicly and as it were officially" (*CCC* 1305).

Through the Sacrament of Confirmation, our whole being—mind, body, and soul—is transformed into a living witness of Jesus Christ, sent into the world to be a messenger of joy, hope, and the Good News of salvation. When we are confirmed, we are equipped to do the work of evangelization in our place and time. Just as the Spirit compels the apostles out of the upper room, the Spirit urges each of us into the great mission of the Church, to proclaim the love of Christ in our words and actions—and by doing so, to build up more fully the kingdom of God.

The invitation implicit in that sacramental grace is to offer everything of who we are to God for the work of evangelization. It means we bring our gifts, talents, and experiences along with us. We use our culture, our values, our intellect, and our will to find new ways to share the story of God's love. We are exactly who we are, and that is exactly who God wants to be Christ's witness.

For the two of us, as Servant of God Thea Bowman so beautifully said, that means we bring our Black (and Tan) selves fully functioning to the Church. We bring the gifts of our culture along with our individuality to both enrich the Church itself and witness to the glory of God alive in our hearts. Our Blackness helps others see God working in the world and in their lives. Our Blackness helps others see how faith can enhance our lives without our giving up our identity. By being exactly who we are, we offer an example of how life in Christ can truly lead to equality without homogeny.

Marcia's Story

"You talk white" were the three words I heard the most while growing up. Living on the north side of Chicago in the '90s, it was probably true. I went to school with white people, had white teachers and white friends. I am sure that to my Black family and friends on the south side of the city I did, in fact, talk white. I was under the impression that my "talking white" was a result of my environment, kind of like Americans who have moved to England. They often develop an affected accent that merges their roots and their current environment.

"You talk white" was meant to be an insult or even dismissive, but there were times when, if I am being honest, I wore it as a badge of pride that enabled me to get what I needed. "Talking white" was my shortcut. It meant that sometimes I didn't have to work so hard to get what I needed, and sometimes my share was larger than half.

Now that I have a greater understanding about how the world works, I can say that what I had been doing since I started inhabiting white spaces was code-switching.

A BLACK HISTORY PRIMER
CODE-SWITCHING

Code-switching is the linguistic practice of switching from one language or dialect to another in conversation. Black Americans who do not speak another language are also known to employ code-switching to successfully navigate interactions with persons of other races that can impact their well-being, career, and financial advancement, even physical survival.

In code-switching, Black people adjust their appearance, speech patterns, and behavior in an effort to make a dominant group feel more comfortable. To give a common example, in the workplace Black employees usually avoid using AAVE (African American Vernacular English) when their supervisors are present and only use it with coworkers and friends. The now-viral video of former president Obama greeting the US Olympic basketball team reflects this type of code-switching.

Code-switching is more than a communication tool. It is a way in which many BIPOC cooperate with the system that privileges European culture norms in order to advance and/or have needs met. Unfortunately, this often demands they become complicit with the racial oppression that dictates compliance with those cultural norms.

Because I grew up on the north side of Chicago surrounded by white people, my speaking voice was always going to be different. But code-switching had less to do with my accent and more to do with my intention. In my college years and early adulthood, I understood that if I wanted opportunities, I would have to diminish my Blackness, mostly for the comfort of white people, so that those who were in between me and a new job, apartment, or relationship would see what I had to offer.

In order to get what I needed and to get ahead, code-switching was something I did early and often in relationships with non-Black people. It was my way of proving that I was worthy of my place in whatever space I was inhabiting. Code-switching kept me safe and included, and it kept me employed. It also kept me in predominantly white spaces, firmly in the white gaze, and kept my true voice from me for a really long time.

It was around the time that George Zimmerman was acquitted for the murder of Trayvon Martin that I realized my ability to code-switch had been more effective than I realized. There were conversations being held in my presence about Black people "knowing our place" and making sure we do what we are told or we would "get what we deserve." I couldn't believe that these conversations were happening in the first place, and I was even more shocked that they were being held around me. Those having these conversations would seemingly excuse their words by saying something like, "Well, not you, Marcia. You're different." When I would inquire as to what made me so different, they would add sheepishly, "You know . . . you're Black, but you're not *really* Black," or "Well, you know, you're not 'ghetto.'"

To my horror, I realized that my code-switching had made those around me so comfortable that it diminished my Blackness in their eyes. It put the worst part of their character on display, while hiding the root of mine. As I grasped the vestiges of my Blackness, I spent the next few years relearning who I was and unlearning who I had taught myself to be. Without realizing it, I had become a tool of my own oppression.

Within a few years I stopped code-switching altogether. I didn't have as many opportunities or relationships with non-Black people, but I did have a better handle on who I am and got comfortable with my voice and my north-side affected accent.

Growing up on the north side of Chicago, I saw the same sign on the doors of a lot of shops and stores: *Hablamos Español*. Up until I was in second or third grade, I had no idea what those words meant; I just knew it said something in Spanish, and I couldn't understand Spanish. Well, that sign wasn't for me. It was for people who spoke Spanish, and it said, "We speak Spanish." It told those that only speak Spanish, "We can serve you here." There was nothing else needed to get service or be seen. These shops communicated that they had resources and would use them to reach others.

I needed to code-switch in my life because, if I was to be seen and served, I had to do the reaching. Others were not trying and/ or willing to reach for me.

In the spirit of celebrating Pentecost in practice, we as a Church should work to understand others. We should put up our metaphorical *Hablamos Español* signs, letting everyone know that we speak their language and they never have to switch to a different code.

Shannon's Story

One of the most important characteristics of witnesses is that they point the way to someone else. St. Paul spells this out in his First Letter to the Corinthians when he warns them against divisions within their local church. "Each of you is saying," he begins, "'I belong to Paul,' or 'I belong to Apollos,' or 'I belong to Cephas,' or 'I belong to Christ.' Is Christ divided? Was Paul crucified for you? Or were you baptized in the name of Paul?" (1 Cor 1:12–13).

He goes on to remind the people of Corinth that he is simply a witness. Christ, he says, "did not send me to baptize but to preach the gospel, and not with the wisdom of human eloquence, so that the cross of Christ might not be emptied of its meaning" (1 Cor 1:17). The work of the witness is to preach the Good News, to lift up the Cross, and ultimately to serve the Spirit of God. When we ignore where the Spirit is moving or we place the importance of human wisdom above the Spirit's work, then we cease to be a witness. Instead, we have placed our own understanding above the will of God.

This insight is especially relevant to me as a light-skinned biracial woman working in the Church. Though I believe my experiences and my voice are important in the work of the Church, I also know that the color of my skin gives me advantages that those with darker skin do not have. For example, I never worry about being accepted when I go into a job interview. I never doubt that people will take me seriously or question my intelligence. When I walk into the room, I don't have to put in any extra work to make sure people will allow me to sit at the table. I am accepted simply because of the color of my skin.

I'll share a very real and raw example from my own life. When I lived in rural Indiana, there was one man in town who spent the summer of 2016 driving around town in his pickup truck covered in Confederate flags. Whenever he encountered large gatherings, he would drive by slowly, staring down people of color who happened to be present and otherwise drawing attention to the symbols he was very clearly displaying. Taken together, these elements communicated clearly to me that I needed to be wary of this man's intentions. I wondered whether the safety of my friends and family who had darker skin might be in jeopardy.

One night that summer, when the kids had gone to bed, I ran over to our local library to pick out a few books before it closed while Eric held down the fort at home. As I came out of the library alone, the same man was driving by in his truck. My body froze, not daring to move a muscle while he drove past, staring at me with a look of disdain and anger that I had never seen before in my life. Had he stopped or circled back to where I was, I would have been alone with no protection and no place to run. The only thing I can remember thinking over and over in those thirty seconds of fear was, *Thank God I look white because otherwise I don't think I'd be going home.*

While this is an extreme example of the advantages of having light skin, it also draws attention in a dramatic way to something most Americans know but don't always wish to acknowledge. The color of our skin really does matter, even if we don't believe it should.

It is not comfortable to acknowledge that some things in my life are easier simply because I was born a certain way. I have worked hard; I have tried to be fair and kind to all people; I am a Christian trying to be like Christ. It makes me feel bad to realize that things are harder for my friends and family with dark skin and that I have been ignorant of that at times. It is difficult to let go of the half-truth that my achievements are my own and that I am the only one responsible for my success. Recognizing my advantages doesn't negate my abilities or achievements; it simply helps me to make sure that others don't have extra hurdles to jump over before they get to my starting line.

But when I refuse to acknowledge the advantages I receive from having light skin, I am not just ignoring the demands of justice, but also quenching the Spirit. God does not limit the work of the Holy Spirit to one type of person, and God shows no partiality to one group of people. The Holy Spirit is present and working among every nation, ethnicity, ability or disability, biological sex, and so on. If I see my experience as more important, more relevant, or more valued by God, I am sinning against the Holy Spirit because I am preventing the voice of the Spirit from being heard from within the whole Church.

If those of us with the advantage of having light skin hold on to that precedence, we close ourselves off to the mystery of God present and moving in the lives of his people. We stop being good witnesses to Christ because we fail to point the way to him wherever he may be found. We, like the Corinthians, place human beings above the Spirit.

However, it is not complicated to make room for the Spirit to move. Just like my family's janky Advent wreath, small steps can make a huge difference. First and foremost, we must listen to and believe the stories of our darker-skinned brothers and sisters. We need to ask them how God is working in their lives and listen to what they need, rather than trying to impose our view from the outside. We can prioritize diversity in music, sacred art, prayer forms, and cultural expressions of the faith. Adding a statue of St. Moses the Black or St. Mark Ji Tianxiang next to St. Thérèse of Lisieux and St. Francis of Assisi does not diminish the beauty of the European expression of our faith; it simply adds some of the beauty of other cultures in our country to our unique American expression of the faith. By prioritizing representation, inclusion, and the undoing of injustices that disadvantage others, we get out of the way of the Holy Spirit without diminishing anything of what the Spirit has already done.

And remember, the Spirit will always, always come whenever we make room.

A BLACK HISTORY PRIMER
COLORISM

One of the major effects of racism on communities of color is the predominance of colorism. Colorism is defined in many ways; put most simply, it means that those in a specific ethnic group with lighter skin are given preferential treatment over those with darker skin. This can occur outside of the ethnic group or within it.

One example of external colorism is found in casting Black actors in TV shows and movies. Historically, leading parts were given to Black actors with medium or light skin, whereas darker actors were typically relegated to supporting roles.

Internalized colorism within an ethnic group is no less insidious than the external pressures. For example, until the mid-twentieth century there were Black churches, nightclubs, and businesses that employed a brown paper bag test, where patrons, congregants, or applicants for employment had to stand next to a brown paper bag for admittance. If their skin was darker than the bag, they were not allowed to enter.

An example of colorism from the twenty-first century is the popularity of skin-lightening and skin-bleaching creams in India, Asia, Africa, and the Americas. Both men and women of color use the creams, which are marketed as additions to a beauty regimen that will make one more "radiant" or "desirable." Using the creams is seen as a way to become more attractive and more successful.

In most cases, the preferential treatment given to lighter-skinned men and women of color is a culturally conditioned, implicit bias upon which we may not have consciously chosen to act. However, colorism is a specific manifestation of racism that we need to uproot from our culture through a committed, sustained effort to represent and celebrate all shades of melanin as beautiful, as well as a concerted effort to set up systems that mitigate and minimize the effects of colorism on those with darker skin. In addition, we must consciously resist acting on this bias and draw attention to its injustice when we see its effects around us.

Distinctly Black, Distinctly Catholic, Truly Universal

The witness of Black Catholics is especially important to the work of the Church in America today. As Black people, we have the gift of our culture as an example of how to transform the worst aspects of our country's history into strength, beauty, and hope. We also have the experience to identify and fight against the pernicious influence of racism in our culture and its institutions. We bring our resilience, persistence, joy, hope, and wisdom to both our country and our Church.

As Catholics, we bring to our Black brothers and sisters and to our nation the gifts given to us in the sacraments, the sustenance of the liturgy, the treasure of Catholic social teaching, a consistent life ethic, and all of the wisdom of Church tradition paired with the witness of the saints. We are uniquely equipped to point the way to Christ, like St. Paul, so that Christ may be all in all.

It is this unique intersection of essential facets of our lives that allows us to posit a model of how our nation can move forward from division into unity that finds its strength in diversity. As Black Catholics, we know the truth of what the Church can be, and how the communion we have in the Body of Christ is the true union toward which we must strive. We also know the value of diversity, of being able to express our unity through our specific cultural expressions and symbols. We know that the Church is the ultimate expression of what God intends for all people—"a great multitude, which no one could count, from every nation, race, people, and tongue" (Rv 7:9), in eternal, ecstatic oneness with each other and with God.

So how, practically, do we get there? How do we translate what is Black and Catholic to what is universal to even those outside the Church? What does it mean to have unity in diversity?

For this, we must look, Church, at who we are and whose we are . . . and bring it to life in our own place and time.

The Church: A Model for Diversity

The Church is a communion of many different cultures, languages, and ethnicities that has managed to be unified in its beliefs, its liturgical practices, and its mission for more than two thousand years. That unity and witness in the midst of such different times, places, and cultures can only be the work of the Holy Spirit. Human organizations do not last across millennia.

So if the Church is our model for diversity in America, it is because the Holy Spirit is animating us toward something bigger. The Church can be a model for unity in diversity because it prefigures the ultimate human goal, beyond the flourishing of our individual nation. The Church can be our model for earthly unity precisely because its unity points to the perfect unity of heaven. As Pope Benedict XVI writes in his encyclical *Caritas in Veritate*, "Earthly activity, when inspired and sustained by charity, contributes to the building of the universal city of God, which is the goal of the history of the human family" (7). Our nation's social, cultural, political, economic, and organizational efforts must be animated, at least for Catholics, by the charity and hope that flow from the Holy Spirit to be truly effective in making changes in our country and in our world.

The lessons we can draw from the life of the Church are many. First, as we learned from Our Lady of Guadalupe, all values must be enculturated. As a country full of diverse cultures, we must recognize that the shared values we have as Americans are not always expressed uniformly across cultures. We can gain new understanding of what these values mean from their different expressions in different cultures, and our deeper understanding can enrich our wider American culture.

For example, the value of hard work is common to our American cultural ethos (turn on a truck commercial and see how many times working hard is mentioned). What the value of hard work looks like is enculturated differently in specific ethnic groups, though. In Black culture one works hard to help support the whole family. European Americans may be more focused on achievement of the individual through hard work. Asian and Hispanic cultures have different motivations for working hard as well. These differences don't negate the shared value of hard work that unites Americans. It means we have taken the value to heart and applied our own cultural lens to the shared universal value. In order to form a more perfect union in our country, we need to realize that compelling uniformity in the way a value is lived will only lead to further division and resentment. Inculturation is not an enemy to unity. The model of the Church's unity shows us that, in fact, inculturation is a cornerstone of true communion grounded in shared belief.

Viewing the Church as a model for diversity also teaches us that there are universal truths that, even if expressed differently, are essential to living in unity. For Catholics these include our shared liturgical practices and prayers (such as liturgies of the

Triduum), the Creed and Church dogmas, the Ten Commandments, the Beatitudes, and the works of mercy. For Americans, we might point to our Constitution; the civil and human rights of all people; the shared commitment to democracy, self-governance, and equality; the belief that individuals can and should determine the course of their own future; and a celebration of cooperation in pursuit of a common cause.

There are certain truths, to borrow from the Declaration of Independence, that must be held as self-evident and certain rights we must all hold to be inalienable if we are to succeed as a nation and, as the preamble to the Constitution says, "ensure the blessings of liberty for ourselves and our posterity." And as Catholics we know that ultimately it is Christ who shows us what those truths, those rights, and those aims are—nothing less than the eternal salvation of every human life through its physical, mental, emotional, and spiritual flourishing.

We can find examples of how to ensure those blessings of liberty in the Church's teaching as well. Our faith tells us that working toward the common good across cultural and religious differences is essential to unity in diversity. One of the lessons we learned from reflecting on Christmas was the importance of making accommodations so that everyone can celebrate together. That is one example of working toward the common good. We also see this in the way the Church dialogues with other religions, the way it embraces the sciences and the arts, and the way it works to provide for people's needs through both works of charity and works promoting justice.

America needs people willing to reach across religious, political, and social barriers to build institutions and promote policies that guarantee the good of every human person regardless of their beliefs, background, or abilities. How policies affect marginalized groups and individuals must be the litmus test for their utility. We must see where people are excluded and work to eliminate that exclusion. We must build a shared American culture that truly values human life in all its forms, in all its stages, and in all its differences.

Unity in diversity must include care for the whole person as an individual as well as part of a community. Benedict XVI, referring us to the wisdom of Pope St. Paul VI, states that "authentic human development concerns the whole of the person in every single dimension" (*Caritas in Veritate* 11). Just as we do spiritual "curl care" to nourish the graces of our baptism, we must also help others nurture and care for themselves as body, mind, and spirit. Unity in diversity means that every person is valued for their inherent dignity and that their spiritual, mental, emotional, and physical well-being is prioritized as part of the common good. It means that cultures are respected and valued. Religious freedom (even the freedom to choose no religion) is respected and valued. Individual consciences are respected and valued. We must see the human person—loved and willed into existence in their own individual beauty by God's own self—as both the subject and object of our national life.

It is imperative that we do not view ourselves at the center of this care for the whole person. Rather, as witnesses to Christ dwelling in the divine life of the Holy Spirit, we see that the human person we must care for is first and foremost the other. To be a truly great nation, to be unified while valuing diversity, we must turn away from the selfishness of rugged individualism and embrace the truth of Ubuntu that Africana people have known for years: "I am because we are." When we focus on the needs of the other, of the community, when we create a "we" first, the individual can be strengthened and nurtured as a whole person. It is simply the truth of the Christian life: we find ourselves by giving ourselves away to others.

Our Whole Selves

When we give ourselves to the service of others, we must bring our whole selves to the task. Just as holding back a part of our self from a spouse in marriage can be detrimental to the health of the relationship, holding back part of who we are from the work God has placed before us will ultimately keep us from succeeding at the work. For the two of us, that means that we bring our whole Black (and Tan) selves to the work of diversity just as we bring our whole selves to the witness we give to Christ.

How do we bring our whole selves to the work of building the kingdom of God in our place and time? Think of it as a bit like a spiritual hokey pokey dance. In the dance we do with the Holy Spirit, we have to jump in with both feet and shake without care for what we look like. Dancing is more fun when we let go of our self-consciousness and give our whole heart, mind, and body to the task.

Bringing our whole selves to the task of building the kingdom means bringing our personality, our gifts, our talents, our likes and dislikes, our hopes, dreams, fears, and hesitations to building a consensus with other people. It means bringing the genius of our cultures, our person, and our experience to the task; respecting and trusting the same in others; and, with love as our first goal, listening to and learning from them as they listen to and learn from us. It means speaking the truth even when it is uncomfortable, but doing so in a way that meets the other where they are rather than where we want them to be. It requires of us a dynamic, flexible way of being in relationship with others, especially those with whom we may not agree. Those who bring their whole selves to God's work are confident in their own wholeness and come as fully functioning humans full of their history, traditions, and hopes. And they do this without taking away from the wholeness of others or inflicting brokenness on them.

That may require work. In our own cases, both of us have needed to learn cultural competencies, go to therapy, seek spiritual direction, and learn our history and traditions from our elders. Being a fully functioning self is a lifelong process. But only when we stand rooted in our own traditions and giftedness can we truly contribute to the life of the Church and the common good in our country to its fullest. It can seem daunting, but it is worth it.

And the beauty of being in a relationship with Jesus is that, even though it may seem daunting, we do not have to do it alone. The Spirit given to the Church at Pentecost and given to each of us in Confirmation has already equipped us with everything we need to be witnesses and to bring our whole selves to the task. God does not ask us to be witnesses and then leave us alone to flounder in solitude. When we are sealed with the Spirit, the Spirit's gifts are stirred up within us so we can have courage when we need it; we can give counsel, share understanding, wisdom, and knowledge when required; we can turn to God in piety, in wonder and awe of his mighty power and mercy. In short, we can be witnesses because God has made us witnesses. God has called us regardless of our ability, and through the power of the sacraments, he has given us the ability to live up to the calling.

We *can* bring our whole selves because God does not keep any good thing from his people. We are already ready to do the work. Will we trust the Holy Spirit and the power of Pentecost enough to go out and do it?

A PENTECOST COMPANION:
THEA BOWMAN

Servant of God Thea Bowman brought her whole self to the Church. For those unfamiliar with this remarkable woman, Thea was a member of the Franciscan Sisters of Perpetual Adoration who was instrumental in leading the liturgical movement among Black Catholics in the 1970s and '80s. Known for her beautiful singing, inspiring preaching, and genuine kindness, Thea was a force for renewal and change within the American Church, affirming the dignity and fullness of Black cultural expressions of the Catholic faith.

Born in 1937 in Canton, Mississippi, Thea grew up in the Black community learning stories and traditions from her elders, especially in her Protestant church. After attending Catholic schools, Thea decided to convert to the faith and at the age of fifteen took steps to join a Franciscan religious community, becoming its only African American member. Throughout her formation and even after her final profession, Sr. Thea was met by racism, prejudice, and mistreatment from people both inside and outside of her order. In spite of this, she found hope in the liturgical renewals of the Second Vatican Council, eventually helping to found the Institute for Black Catholic Studies at Xavier University in New Orleans, which is a cultural center for Black Catholics even to this day.

Though she is remembered most often for her courageous and moving speech to the US Bishops' Conference in 1989 that we quoted above, Thea Bowman was more than a powerful orator. She was someone who witnessed to the love of Christ through her joy, through her work to bring about justice and equality in the Church, and through her willingness to call the Church to account when it needed to be reminded of its mission. Her wisdom, graciousness, grit, and giftedness exemplify how we can bring our whole self to the Church and to the world—not sacrificing our identity in order to assimilate, but rather making the world more holy through the sharing of our faith and personal genius. Servant of God Thea Bowman brought herself fully functioning to the Church and to the world. May we all imitate her strength and be just as much of a gift to the Church as she was.

REFLECTION **QUESTIONS**

1. Shannon and Marcia talk about the importance of being witnesses throughout this chapter. What unique gifts do you bring to your witness to Christ?

2. Marcia discusses giving up code-switching between cultures. Have there been times in your life when you changed your behavior in order to fit in? How did it affect you?

3. Why do you think Shannon says that focusing on representation and inclusion is so important for being witnesses to the work of the Holy Spirit?

4. How does viewing the Church as a model for diversity help us create a framework for working toward racial justice in America?

5. What are some obstacles you face in bringing your whole self to God's work? How can you better trust that God has equipped you to do the work placed before you?

10

THE NECK OF THE CHURCH
The Feast of Christ the King

If you were to draw up an organizational chart for the worldwide Church, it would be pretty easy to map out the power dynamics. The pope sits at the head of the Church with the bishops and provincials of religious orders below him, followed by the clergy in the various parishes, missions, and communities around the world. What is apparent, at least from the outside, is that laypeople of every stripe—and women in particular—seem to be missing from the organizational chart. In parishes, dioceses, and the Vatican, ordained men are at the head of the Church. As women, and particularly as women of color, we don't often see people like us making decisions for the institutional Church, even as it is primarily laywomen (and men!) doing the bulk of the day-to-day work of ministry at its parishes.

In dealing with these sticky issues of gender and leadership in the Church, we like to turn to one of the great wise women of our time: Maria Portokalos, the mother in the classic rom-com *My Big Fat Greek Wedding.* Early in the movie as Toula, the main character, is trying to persuade her father Gus to pay for college classes, she finds him stubborn and (from Toula's perspective) stuck in the Stone Age. She turns to her mother Maria in tears and expresses her frustration with Gus's attitude toward women and his insistence that the man is the head of the house.

Maria replies with the humor and wisdom one would expect from a woman who knows her husband well after decades of marriage.

"The man," Maria says to her daughter, "is the head. But the woman is the neck. And she can turn the head any way she wants."[1]

Now, we don't believe in manipulating our priests and bishops—that certainly would not be holy or righteous. However, we do believe that, if the clergy are at the head of the institutional church, as laity we are—as Maria says—the neck that turns the head. While the clergy are ordained to be servant leaders and to guide the Church through the charisms of their vocation, they are given this task so that the laity, who constitute the overwhelming majority of the Church, may live out their vocation to be the Body of Christ living and active in the world.

Gaudium et Spes, the "Pastoral Constitution on the Church in the Modern World," explicates this idea more fully. *Gaudium et Spes* is a solemn proclamation of the magisterium in an ecumenical council (so like, the most important and binding kind of Church document—you know, super-duper important Catholic stuff). "Secular duties and activities," the document states,

> belong properly although not exclusively to [laypeople]. . . . [The laity] should also know that it is generally the function of their well-formed Christian conscience to see that the divine law is inscribed in the life of the earthly city; from priests they may look for spiritual light and nourishment. Let the [layperson] not imagine that his pastors are always such experts, that to every problem which arises, however complicated, they can readily give him a concrete solution, or even that such is their mission. Rather, enlightened by Christian wisdom and giving close attention to the teaching authority of the Church, let the [layperson] take on his own distinctive role. . . . Since they have an active role to play in the whole life of the Church, laymen are not only bound to penetrate the world with a Christian spirit,

but are also called to be witnesses to Christ in all things in the midst of human society. (43)

To state things slightly more succinctly (if less eloquently), the role of the laity is to be the hands and feet of Christ in the world, working and living alongside our neighbors, evangelizing them through our virtue, good works, and steadfast hope. The clergy are there to help us, guide us in our relationship with God, and provide us spiritual care so that we can build the kingdom of God in our homes, neighborhoods, workplaces, and everywhere else we meet others. It is our work to transform our economies, schools, political systems, literature, music, movies, and so on.

In this vocation it is the laity who encounter the "joys and the hopes, the griefs and the anxieties of . . . this age" (1). In turn we bring these to our pastors, our bishops, and the global Church, speaking to the "head" in trust and with shared faith that our questions will find answers in Christ, who is the true (and, ultimately, the only) head of the Church. In turning the Church's attention to the cares of our place and time, we act as the neck, moving the head in the directions where its attention is needed most.

This is especially poignant to us as women of color, who serve the People of God as leaders in the Church. We have often been the ones in the background organizing, teaching, cajoling, pray-ing, crying, laughing, and making the everyday business of the Church happen. Because of our gender and our race, we have experienced discrimination in practice even when the truth of Church teaching affirms our equal citizenship in the heavenly kingdom and in the pews. We know we have a special role in the Church to keep our Church moving in and out of the pews. Women have a purpose and a place in the Body of Christ. We are half of the Body of Christ, and our voices are essential to the work of turning the head and telling it where to go (it also helps that we are strong and flexible).

Our experience has taught us that women's wisdom is critical to the Church. Women, both lay and religious, need to be leaders in every aspect of Church life that does not require ordination. Women (and lay men, too!) need to be in positions of authority, to make decisions about the communities in which they live, the parishes where they worship, and the mission of the local church. People of color, especially, need to be represented in leadership at least in proportion to their presence within the Church. And these roles are not to be focused inward on the Church itself, but rather outward on sustaining and forwarding the mission of the Church through the work of evangelization and social justice. In short, the head of the Church needs to give the neck room to point it in the direction that will allow it to see the whole picture.

The Solemnity of Christ the King speaks especially to this dynamic within the Body of Christ. At the very end of the liturgical year, we rejoice in Christ, the Head of the Body, who has entered into heaven. Where the Head has gone, we know that the Body will follow. We end our liturgical cycle by acknowledging the nature of the kingdom of Christ: the reign of God is always here-but-not-yet. It is a feast that is made for the laity who live in the midst of the world as citizens of both our earthly cities and the New Jerusalem that is to come.

Christ the King is a feast for the neck of the Church because it is a feast of here-but-not-yet for a people that is here-but-not-yet. It is a feast of the King whose kingdom is in our hands because we are his hands for others. It is a feast to turn heads to the voices that are not yet sitting at the table so that ears may hear those whom Christ the King came to save. Christ the King is the feast for the end of the year and for the unfolding of the kingdom of God.

Marcia's Story

Let me start by saying that I really don't know anything about Clint Eastwood. I just know a story that I heard about him when I was in college. I don't remember why the subject came up, but at some point the conversation turned to Clint Eastwood, and this guy would not stop singing the praises of one Mr. Eastwood. He told us Eastwood was a living legend who didn't let anyone push him around. "He didn't let people tell him when he was done making movies," my friend said. "And when they told him that he was too old, he just took matters into his own hands!"

At this point, we were all listening. We wanted to know more. He went on to tell us that when Clint heard the word "no," he set out to prove that he could do everything he was told he couldn't. He put up the money for a movie, he directed it, and he even starred in it. "And then he won an Oscar for it, and he showed them all!"

"Yeah!" we all agreed. I, who had just learned that Eastwood was not, in fact, the same guy who played Moses (that was Charlton Heston), was oh so proud of him and his story of triumph. To hear that random dude tell it, Clint Eastwood was the underdog who got to keep the bone.

I am telling you this fantastical story that I can't seem to fact-check because it made me feel less alone.

There have been many times in my life when I have been told no, felt excluded or underserved, and had to either set a different course or create my own. That day in the dorm lounge, I learned that even Clint Eastwood had to challenge adversity. And he was Clint Eastwood!

From that point on, I had a bit more wind in my sails if I was unable to get a need met in my life or struggled to find belonging in different settings. I also knew what I had to do: I would have to Clint Eastwood it! Yes, I really said this, if only to myself for the first couple of years, and yes, I made an Oscar-winning director's name a verb. And yes, I am well aware that there are more suitable role models for young Black women, but Clint's name as a verb has been living in my head rent-free for at least two decades.

In the last five years I started sharing my secret verb with others when we were working together on a project in an effort to explain my vision. So far I have shared this story (which could very well be folklore) with the people I worked with to build an after-school program, a peer ministry team, a number of food drives, a shenanigans-filled podcast, and a national organization committed to antiracism and a consistent life ethic.

I have Clint Eastwooded a lot in my life, and I am not done yet. Turning the head is all fine and good for a while, but if we are going to grow as a Church and I am going to grow as a person, then I need to keep creating spaces and cultivating resources for those we are not reaching. My neck muscle needs to be exercised, and if I need Dirty Harry's help, so be it. He also knew how to get stuff done.

Shannon's Story

A few years ago when our parish priests were attending the yearly convocation for the priests of the diocese, I was tasked with leading some Communion services at the times when daily Mass was normally scheduled. The person leading a Communion service can give a reflection on the scripture readings for the day.

One day, the gospel reading happened to be the story of Martha and Mary, where Martha tries to get Jesus to send Mary back to the kitchen. As any good former theology student would do, I looked at some Bible commentaries and other sources before praying and writing what I hoped would be a meaningful reflection for those attending the service.

The reflection I gave centered on the cultural context of the story. In first-century Judaism, not only were women expected to help in the preparations for the banquet that Jesus would have attended, but their role as hostess would have been seen as their path to righteousness. Mary was not only leaving Martha in a lurch; she was doing the opposite of what a holy Jewish woman should do.

In addition, the act of sitting at the feet of a rabbi was a public declaration. By sitting at the rabbi's feet, one was publicly declaring oneself a disciple who would learn from him and follow his teachings instead of any other's. And if the rabbi allowed someone to sit at his feet, it meant he was accepting them as a disciple who would learn his way of teaching and, one day, become a rabbi as well. So this action of Mary's was a very public act of discipleship in the midst of the community.

But there's a problem with that. In first-century Judaism, only men could be disciples and only men could be rabbis. Both Mary and Jesus were breaking all the rules.

It is a story that begs us to consider several questions. What is required of us to be holy? What limits do we impose on discipleship ourselves, as opposed to what Jesus asks of us? How can we imitate the radical discipleship of Mary, regardless of our biological sex? It is a story where the perspective of women is essential for understanding its full meaning. It is about *so much more* than being too busy to listen to Jesus.

After the Communion service ended, a group of women approached me, most in the age range of sixty years and up. They expressed to me how meaningful it was to hear that interpretation of the scriptural story and how that was the first time in their lives that they had heard anyone describe Martha and Mary in that way. They commented on how insightful it was to hear someone speak about that scripture from a woman's perspective.

Now, I first heard this commentary on Martha and Mary when I was working on my undergraduate theology degree, likely when I was about twenty years old. As a woman, there was much I could relate to in both Martha's story and Mary's. As these women stood beaming over my words (which were really just drawn from a standard Bible commentary), I was flabbergasted. What would it be like to go through my whole life without hearing my perspective once from the pulpit or a professor's mouth? It made me want to shout out in anger at all of the beauty that these women had missed because their experience was not valued in the interpretation of scripture, especially from those teaching the Catholic faith. How long had they, and the men around them, missed out on the ways God was speaking to the Church through that story and others by not considering that gender was a key element to understanding the whole?

But do not despair. There is more to the story.

About a year later, I was sitting in the pew during Mass on the Third Sunday of Lent for the First Scrutiny of the RCIA catechumens. The gospel reading for the First Scrutiny, regardless of the year, is always the story of Jesus meeting the Samaritan woman at the well. When our associate pastor began his homily, he focused on an interpretation of the story in which the five husbands of the Samaritan woman can be understood to represent the five gods worshipped by the Samaritans instead of the one God of the Jews. In an instant, my face broke into a smile.

Why, you ask?

This particular interpretation of the woman at the well was first posited by a female biblical scholar, Sandra M. Schneiders, in 2003. This story had been interpreted in many ways through the two millennia of the Church's history, but a woman who brought her experience to its interpretation, who refused to see the story only as one about sexual sin and shame, helped the whole Church dive deeper into its meaning. Her contribution had nothing to do with whether or not she was ordained. It had everything to do with her being a woman. She was a neck turning heads toward a new understanding of scripture and of God.

By sharing her theological reflections, this priest did exactly what I so wanted for the Church—bringing the essential experiences and contributions of women smack-dab into the middle of the life of the Church . . . right where they belong.

The Neck That Turns the Head

There's a common adage that says, "If you want something done, ask a busy person" . . . who is probably a woman . . . working for the Church.

In all seriousness, the unseen contributions of laypeople (and religious!) have been at the heart of the Church's history from day one. Even though they have not always been written down in the history books, the contributions of the laity have been a bulwark of Church life since the Resurrection. We have always brought our gifts to the Church and found spaces for them to share the love of Christ with others. In twenty-first-century America, our gifts are urgently needed, especially the gifts of women and people of color. We need to take up our role as the neck of the Church to turn the head toward the most urgent needs of our time.

If the Church is called into every community in the world, it needs people from within those communities to guide and direct its efforts. It is the people in the midst of each community who know its hopes, fears, needs, and riches. Being the neck means being able to identify those hopes and fears and point the head toward how the gifts of the Church can bring Christ into those places. This means that where the Church is making decisions, input is needed from many different voices, especially those most affected. It means that the people making decisions for a community need to reflect the makeup of the community they serve. Basically, being the neck means we invite stakeholders into the process and also use the genius of individuals and cultures to speak of Jesus Christ in a way they will be most apt to hear it. As the neck, we must support and strengthen the head to live the mission of the Church on the most local level possible (the principle of subsidiarity) with the broadest representation we can invite.

People of color and women have unique insight into this task. As we discussed with reference to Our Lady of Guadalupe, women are most often the culture bearers for the community. This perspective, as well as our perspective on living in the world as women, has direct bearing on the task of how the Church serves the whole community. People of color are needed in Church leadership, too, because of our experiences of marginalization within American history and the insights that our various cultures can bring outside of the European norms that tend to dominate our country and the American Church. We can speak best to how to dismantle the systems of discrimination, racism, and injustice in our own communities without eroding the values that belong singularly to our individual cultures.

In twenty-first-century America, the neck must also direct the head to look outside of our church walls. We need worship, prayer, and community within the church walls, but discipleship also requires putting our faith into action. Through both charitable deeds and works of justice, Catholics must be in the streets working to address people's urgent needs and to improve their lives through institutional change. We must consider deeply what attitudes and actions we take in politics, economics, social life, the arts, medicine, and everything else. Decisions as simple as what products we buy at the grocery store have long-lasting effects on communities around the globe. As Pope Benedict XVI says in *Caritas in Veritate*, "Locating resources, financing, production, consumption and all the other phases in the economic cycle inevitably have moral implications. *Thus every economic decision has a moral consequence*" (37).

If we are people who love and serve Christ the King, we must be people who build his kingdom. While it is important to our spiritual lives to participate in Bible studies, book clubs, Rosary groups, and so on, building the kingdom of God is more than prayer and study. Those things sustain us and refresh us, strengthening the neck. But the kingdom of God is about *doing*. It is about taking the love we have nourished through prayer and study into the streets. It requires us to not only meet the immediate needs of the community through charitable works but also ask the question of why those needs exist in the first place. When we have answered the why, like good stewards of any kingdom, we must then look for long-term solutions to those needs by addressing their roots within our institutions and the systems that make up society. The neck must point the head to both the gaping wounds that require immediate attention and the diseases that require diagnosis and long-term treatment. In short, working for the kingdom means seeing to both the here and the not-yet.

Recognizing the here-and-not-yet also keeps us from forgetting that we work for Christ's kingdom, not our own. It is Jesus whose glory is revealed by our good works and our accomplishments. It is God who brings about transformation; we simply cooperate with the Lord. We will never fully accomplish all of the work of the kingdom in our time—we will only plant seeds and tend those that others planted before us. We are laying a foundation for the next generation of the Church to build upon.

The wisdom of our Black elders is especially meaningful to understanding our role as the neck. As we pointed out in the chapter on Lent, the elders have taught us over and over again that the work of justice and equality, of the true flourishing of Black people and Black culture, is the work of generations. That truth is what gets us through the hard times when we despair, and what delights us in the good times when freedom wins another victory. Good or bad, we endure and rejoice because we know that the next generation will see something better. We know that the flourishing of all is worth the struggle. And we know that the success of our times will benefit not just us, but our children's children's children. This is a lesson for the neck of the Church. It helps us understand our role and to know that—even though there is urgency to the works of charity and justice—God's kingdom is the work of generations, and it is God's work. "We are workers, not master builders; ministers, not messiahs. We are prophets of a future not our own."[2]

Let's Get to Work

Reflecting on this final feast of the liturgical year, on what it means to be the neck of the Church and to build the kingdom, we see that there is work to do. God gives the task of building the kingdom to every generation, to speak of the hope, love, and joy of Jesus Christ to our place and time. We have work to do.

Each of us brings different gifts, talents, and even weaknesses to this work. Some of us are single, some married. Some of us are artists, some engineers, construction workers, retail workers, theologians, small-business owners, stay-at-home parents, retirees, aging, growing, with varied physical abilities and every situation in between. We all have different work to do.

We don't presume to tell you what work God is calling you to, but we do have some ideas for how to discern it. One of the methods we find most helpful in our own lives is a four-step cycle of reflection. Like the familiar "See-Judge-Act" method that many apply through the prism of Catholic social teaching, it is a cycle that moves from action to reflection and back again.

First, we take an *experience* we have had—for example, working at a local food pantry—and *examine* it. Looking at what happened and bringing the experience to prayer, we start to ask some fundamental questions. What was the experience? What was the need? What was the cause? What were the obstacles? What can be done to reduce or remove the need? Reflecting and praying with our experiences, we begin to see where God is present within them, what meaning we can draw from them, and what actions we might begin to take.

To go back to our example of the food pantry, we may notice a preponderance of families with young children. In discovering this reality, our reflection and prayer may lead us to search out why this particular group is experiencing food insecurity. Perhaps we, like Servant of God Dorothy Day, have seen the hidden face of Christ in those seeking assistance. We may feel a pull to do more than stock shelves to help alleviate the need in the community and to take steps to change whatever circumstances may be causing so many young families to seek assistance.

Once we have examined the experience, we can begin to *integrate* it into our own lives. The experience and the meaning we draw from it can become part of our own story, shaping who we are, what we value, and how we view the world. We take what we have learned and use it to transform our person.

Turning once again to the food pantry example, we may find that through our reflections we have discovered a passion for providing people access to fresh, healthy food no matter their economic circumstances. This reveals to us a value we have (ensuring all people can have full, healthy lives) and also the kind of person we want to be (someone who works for the good of others). By integrating these insights into our understanding of ourselves, we begin to see how we can change and grow.

Finally, we move from integration into *action*. Our new values, insights, and connection to the Lord motivate us to act in alignment with those values and insights. Perhaps we move from working at the food pantry to working with organizations that eliminate food deserts[3] or that connect farmers directly to consumers through community-supported agriculture programs.[4]

The cycle of *experience-examine-integrate-act* works for everyone in every line of work, every stage of life, and every community in the world. It allows us to bring our Catholic Shine to the everyday stuff of our lives, to find God in the midst of our experiences and listen to what he is calling us to do. It can be applied to experiences regarding race, culture, faith, parenting, friendship, work, and everything else in human life. It allows us to embrace our role as the neck of the Church because it gives us the opportunity to reflect on what experiences mean for us as individuals as well as a larger society. It allows us to discern the work of the Holy Spirit in our own lives and to process where the neck needs to help direct the head. It works for the conference table and the kitchen table. It is a method for looking for Christ our King in our midst so we might join him there in establishing his reign.

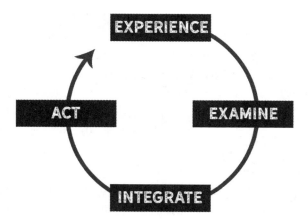

It is time for us to get to work, to do whatever it is we can do to bring out the reign of Christ our King. Doing the work—though not simple—is easily summed up: "Be merciful, just as your Father is merciful" (Lk 6:36).

Building the kingdom, creating unity in diversity, bringing about justice and peace—doing the work—is simply to accept the merciful love of God for ourselves and to imitate it with every person we meet with no exceptions, no limits, and no reservations. God's mercy is the only thing that can overcome the divisions we see all around us. To quote Pope Francis, "God's mercy can make even the driest land become a garden, and can restore life to dry bones. . . . Let us be renewed by God's mercy, let us be loved by Jesus, let us enable the power of his love to transform our lives too; and let us become agents of this mercy, channels through which God can water the earth, protect all creation and make justice and peace flourish."[5]

The work of building the kingdom and bringing about unity in diversity is not a one-and-done thing. Learning cultural competencies, working against racism and all other attacks on human life, seeking justice and peace: all of these are spiritual practices that require self-care and self-discipline. Like any form of spiritual development and faith formation, this work is a lifelong journey.

At the beginning of this journey through the liturgical year, we invited you to pull up a chair at our table, to learn and grow with us as we seek to find a model in the Church of a way forward in America. We are grateful you have joined us and hope that, like the two of us, you have found hope for a world in which every life can flourish and grow without exceptions.

Now, however, it is time for us to leave this table and to encourage you to continue to do the work wherever you may find yourself. Continue your lifelong journey of learning to appreciate and celebrate all people and the gifts each culture brings to our Church and to our world. There are many other voices to learn from and many other cultures that have wisdom to teach our Church. It's time to pick up your chair, sit down at a new table, and start learning from someone else.

It's time to get to work.

A KINGLY COMPANION:
POPE ST. JOHN *XXIII*

Most of us know Pope St. John XXIII as the pope who called the Second Vatican Council, initiating a renewal of the Church as it adapted to the technological age. This alone would solidify him as a historic figure in Church history. But what makes John XXIII the best companion for the Feast of Christ the King is the way his life consistently demonstrates an openness to listen to the Holy Spirit and to respond with courage, humor, and zeal for doing the Lord's will.

John XXIII was born Angelo Giuseppe Roncalli in Bergamo, Italy, in 1881. He earned a doctorate in theology and was ordained a priest in 1905, serving as secretary to the bishop until that man's death in 1914 just as World War I overtook Europe.

Roncalli served as a stretcher bearer on the front, seeing firsthand the horror of this new type of warfare waged by machines at the command of bureaucrats far away from the front lines.

At the end of the war and of his service in the army in 1919, Roncalli was personally chosen by Pope Benedict XV to serve as the Italian president of the Society for the Propagation of the Faith, until he was appointed a papal nuncio in 1925. As nuncio he served in Turkey and Greece working to improve relations with the Muslim communities in those regions. When Hitler established the Nazi government in Germany in 1935, Roncalli was disturbed by the anti-Semitic racism pervading Europe and worked to issue transit visas to Jewish men and women to help them escape Nazi persecution. It is estimated he saved the lives of more than 24,000 Jews.

In 1944, at the end of the war, he was named papal nuncio to Paris to oversee the removal of clergy who collaborated with the Nazi regime. He served in Paris until he was named patriarch of Venice and installed as a cardinal.

Roncalli chose the name John when he was elected pope in 1958. During his papacy, John XXIII was extremely popular for his reforms of the Vatican, his sense of humor, and his willingness to be among the people. He also consistently worked to promote peace and disarmament, having seen the aftermath of two wars within his lifetime. The culmination of this work for peace was his famous encyclical on the promotion of peace, *Pacem in Terris*, written just before his death in 1963.

Pope St. John XXIII is the perfect companion for the end of our journey through the liturgical year because his holiness, faith, and goodwill reflect the truth of what each of us is called to be—men and women who listen to the Spirit, who work with joy for others, and who bring to our day and time the kingdom of God under the reign of Christ the King.

REFLECTION **QUESTIONS**

1. What are some ways that you have seen the laity act as the neck of the Church in your community?

2. In what parts of your life do you need to imitate Marcia and "Clint Eastwood this"?

3. Shannon talks about the importance of bringing women's experience to the life of the Church. Why do you think it's important for diverse voices to be included in the worship, teaching, and decision-making of the Church?

4. Marcia and Shannon present the cycle of *experience-examine-integrate-act* as a method of discernment. In what situations in your own life can you see this method being helpful?

5. What is one way you feel called to continue to work on building the kingdom of God in your particular vocation?

ACKNOWLEDGMENTS

Special thanks go to the team at Ave Maria Press for helping this book go from a phrase in a podcast episode to a published work. We are especially grateful to our editor, Heidi Hess Saxton, for her care, input, and belief that *Fat Luther, Slim Pickin's* could come alive on the page.

Thanks to all of our *Plaid Skirts and Basic Black* podcast listeners who have been with us on this crazy journey and who join us ten weeks in a row, twice a year, to amplify our voices in the Church.

Thank you to our parents (and Nannie), who have given us the gift of life, encouragement in faith, and a passion for loving others. We are grateful for all of our family members who give us unconditional love each day, and especially for Eric, who corralled children for many, many Zoom calls in the writing process.

Above all, we thank our Lord and Savior Jesus Christ, who has given us more than we could ever ask for or imagine. May we always keep our hearts and minds fixed on you.

NOTES

INTRODUCTION

1. In this book we will use multiple terms to describe people of African descent. When we use the word "black" as a descriptor for someone's appearance, it will always be lowercase, like any other adjective. When we are referring to Black American culture or Black Americans descended from Africans kidnapped into forced labor, we will capitalize the word. We use the phrase "of African descent" or the word "Africana" to describe all people of the African diaspora around the world.

2. Francis, "Address of His Holiness to the Thai Government" (Inner Santi Maitri Hall of the Government House, November 20, 2019), Vatican website, https://www.vatican.va/content/francesco/en/speeches/2019/november/documents/papa-francesco_20191121_autorita-thailandia.html.

2. "WHAT ARE YOU?" AND OTHER RUDE QUESTIONS

1. A quick Black culture tip for our readers: the title "G" has to be given to an individual by someone else. We can't claim to be G ourselves—we have to let someone else give us that praise. So, don't be offended at all if someone calls you a G, but don't be surprised if you get lots of weird looks by calling yourself one.

2. The symbols discussed here are drawn from a variety of sources including the website of the Basilica of Our Lady of Guadalupe, various scholarly books on Our Lady, and multiple reputable Catholic magazines and newspapers. While there is some debate about the meaning of Our Lady of Guadalupe among the Mexican people, we tried to focus on those symbols that are agreed upon by scholars and others who study the apparition closely.

3. Gregory I, "Letter to Abbot Mellitus," Internet History Sourcebooks Project, Fordham University, https://sourcebooks.fordham.edu/source/greg1-mellitus.txt.

3. CHITLINS, THE TEMPS, AND FAT LUTHER

1. The Great Migration is the period from 1916 to 1970 when approximately six million Black Americans migrated from the rural South to the urban centers of the Northeast, West, and Midwest looking for improved economic opportunities and freedom from the oppressive laws of the Jim Crow South.

2. This is a delicious layered dessert consisting of a crumbled-pretzel base, cream-cheese fluff, and strawberry jello. This probably didn't need a note, but we really thought you needed to know how delicious it is—especially to honor Shannon's poor aunt who has been forced to make it for the past three decades for every family holiday celebration.

5. THAT CATHOLIC SHINE

1. The "Ordinary" in Ordinary Time is from the word "ordinal," meaning "counted," not "ordinary" in the common understanding in the English language. Nevertheless, Ordinary Time refers to the "normal" or "regular" experience of the liturgical year. When referring to Ordinary Time, we assume both the proper liturgical definition and its place as the norm for our worship during the year.

6. REFINER'S FIRE

1. As they say on *Dragnet*, the story you are about to hear is true. Names have been changed to protect the innocent.

2. While Fr. Tolton was long recognized as the first priest of African descent in America (ordained in 1886), he was actually preceded in the 1850s by Bishop James Healy and Fr. Patrick Healy, the sons of an Irish immigrant father and a Black mother.

Since the Healys were light-skinned, they "passed" as white, and their heritage was unknown until the 1960s.

7. IT LOOKS LIKE YOU'RE LEANING

1. *While You Were Sleeping*, written by Daniel G. Sullivan and Fredric Lebow, dir. Jon Turteltaub (1995; Burbank, CA: Walt Disney Studios Motion Pictures, 2010), DVD.

8. MADE FOR SUCH A TIME

1. These denominations are the National Baptist Convention, the National Baptist Convention of America, the Progressive National Convention, the African Methodist Episcopal Church, the African Methodist Episcopal Zion Church, the Christian Methodist Episcopal Church, and the Church of God in Christ.

2. John Paul II, "Address to the Representatives of Rural Australia at the Festival Centre" (Melbourne, November 30, 1986), Vatican website, https://www.vatican.va/content/john-paul-ii/en/speeches/1986/november/documents/hf_jp-ii_spe_19861130_industrie-adelaide-australia.html.

10. THE NECK OF THE CHURCH

1. *My Big Fat Greek Wedding*, written by Nia Vardalos, dir. Joel Zwick (2002; New York: IFC Films, 2007), DVD.

2. John Dearden, "Prophets of a Future Not Our Own" (speech written by Ken Untener, given in Detroit, 1979), USCCB website, https://www.usccb.org/prayer-and-worship/prayers-and-devotions/prayers/prophets-of-a-future-not-our-own.

3. Food deserts are geographic areas where access to affordable, healthy food options, especially produce, is limited or nonexistent because there are no grocery stores within convenient traveling distance.

4. In community-supported agriculture programs, or CSAs, members of the community support local farms by buying a share of the farm's production before the growing season. In return,

those who invest in the farm receive regular distribution of the farm's products throughout the year.

5. Francis, "Urbi et Orbi Message" (Rome, March 31, 2012), Vatican website, https://www.vatican.va/content/francesco/en/messages/urbi/documents/papa-francesco_20130331_urbi-et-orbi-pasqua.html.

SELECTED BIBLIOGRAPHY

Benedict XVI. *Caritas in Veritate*. Washington, DC: USCCB, 2009.

Bowman, Thea. "Address to the US Bishops' Conference." Washington, DC, June 1989. USCCB website, https://www.usccb.org/issues-and-action/cultural-diversity/african-american/resources/upload/Transcript-Sr-Thea-Bowman-June-1989-Address.pdf.

The Catholic Study Bible. 3rd ed. New York: Oxford University Press, 2016.

Dearden, John. "Prophets of a Future Not Our Own." Speech written by Ken Untener, given in Detroit, 1979. USCCB website, https://www.usccb.org/prayer-and-worship/prayers-and-devotions/prayers/prophets-of-a-future-not-our-own.

Francis. "Address of His Holiness to the Thai Government." Inner Santi Maitri Hall of the Government House, November 20, 2019. Vatican website, https://www.vatican.va/content/francesco/en/speeches/2019/november/documents/papa-francesco_20191121_autorita-thailandia.html.

———. "Urbi et Orbi Message." March 31, 2013. Vatican website, https://www.vatican.va/content/francesco/en/messages/urbi/documents/papa-francesco_20130331_urbi-et-orbi-pasqua.html.

Gregory I. "Letter to Abbot Mellitus." Internet History Sourcebooks Project, Fordham University. https://sourcebooks.fordham.edu/source/greg1-mellitus.txt.

John Paul II. "Address to the Representatives of Rural Australia at the Festival Centre." Melbourne, November 30, 1986. Vatican website, https://www.vatican.va/content/john-paul-ii/en/speeches/1986/november/documents/hf_jp-ii_spe_19861130_industrie-adelaide-australia.html.

My Big Fat Greek Wedding. Written by Nia Vardalos, directed
    by Joel Zwick. 2002; New York: IFC Films, 2007. DVD.
Vatican Council II. *Gaudium et Spes.* 1965. Vati-
    can website, https://www.vatican.va/archive/
    hist_councils/ ii_vatican_council/documents/
    vat-ii_const_19651207_gaudium-et-spes_en.html.
While You Were Sleeping. Written by Daniel G. Sullivan and
    Fredric Lebow, directed by Jon Turteltaub. 1995; Burbank,
    CA: Walt Disney Studios Motion Pictures, 2010. DVD.

FURTHER READING
AND OTHER RESOURCES

Interested in learning more about some of the topics we covered in this book? Here are just a few introductory books, films, and articles to dive deeper into Black culture, diversity, equity, and inclusion, and Catholicism. As some of these resources come from secular sources, they may not reflect the fullness of Church teaching, but they are valuable resources nonetheless. We encourage you to bring them into dialogue with the wisdom of the Church.

INTRODUCTION

Psych. Created by Steve Franks, featuring James Roday Rodriguez and Dulé Hill. 2006; New York: NBCUniversal Media, 2014. DVD.

One of our favorite TV shows of all time! Shawn and Gus are us; we are Shawn and Gus (kudos to you if you can figure out which of us identifies with each character!). From the ridiculous nicknames to the constant pop-culture references, *Psych* is a delight from episode one to the series finale.

Francis. *Fratelli Tutti*. Washington, DC: US Conference of Catholic Bishops, 2020.

If you want to know what Pope Francis means when he talks about unity and diversity, you need to read *Fratelli Tutti*. His discussion of the encounter between cultures is especially relevant to those who want to work toward racial justice in the Church and beyond.

1. JANKY LITURGICAL

Gould, Meredith. *The Catholic Home: Celebrations and Traditions for Holidays, Feast Days, and Every Day*. New York: Doubleday, 2004.

Meredith Gould's book on liturgical traditions to bring to one's house is perfect for those who want to do liturgical living but have no idea where to start. It's especially helpful for those of us whose efforts to do liturgical traditions at home may be a little more slapdash than those who have the skills to put together pretty decor, appropriately themed menus, and coordinated crafts.

Gates, Henry Louis, Jr. *The African Americans: Many Rivers to Cross.* 2013; New York: Public Broadcasting Service, 2013. Streaming Video.

This documentary by Dr. Gates, a Harvard professor and one of the leading scholars of African American history, is one of the best overviews of Black American history one can find. A six-episode miniseries, it begins in the sixteenth century with the black Spanish conquistadores and spans US history up to the election of President Barack Obama. We can't recommend it enough.

2. "WHAT ARE YOU?" AND OTHER RUDE QUESTIONS

Valeriano, Antonio. *Nican Mopohua.* Ca. 1560. Dominican Sisters of Springfield, Illinois, website. https://springfieldop.org/wp-content/uploads/nican_mopohua_english.pdf.

You may have heard the story of Our Lady of Guadalupe, but it is absolutely worth reading the sixteenth-century text that records the event. Thanks to the Dominican sisters, you can find it in English, online, and for free!

Jackson, Lauren Michele. *White Negroes: When Cornrows Were in Vogue . . . and Other Thoughts on Cultural Appropriation.* Boston: Beacon Press, 2020.

Jackson's book is a witty, thought-provoking reflection on cultural appropriation of Black ingenuity and how we can all be better at thoughtful engagement with other cultures.

Pope Gregory I. "Letter to Abbot Mellitus." Internet History Sourcebooks Project, Fordham University. https://sourcebooks. fordham.edu/source/greg1-mellitus.txt.

For all you fellow theology nerds out there from Shannon: This short letter from Gregory the Great was vital for the missionary work of the Church and has wisdom for our efforts to evangelize today.

International Theological Commission. *Faith and Inculturation*. 1988. Vatican website, https://www.vatican. va/roman_curia/congregations/cfaith/cti_documents/ rc_cti_1988_fede-inculturazione_en.html.

Want to know more about what the Church means by inculturation? The best place to start is this 1988 document from the International Theological Commission.

3. CHITLINS, THE TEMPS, AND FAT LUTHER

Twitty, Michael W. *The Cooking Gene: A Journey through African American Culinary History in the Old South*. New York: HarperCollins, 2017.

Culinary historian Michael Twitty explores the intersection of race, history, and food in this essential reading on the history of African American cuisine.

Lukas, Albert G., and Jessica B. Harris. *Sweet Home Cafe Cookbook: A Celebration of African American Cooking*. Washington, DC: Smithsonian Books, 2018.

The *Sweet Home Cafe Cookbook* is the official cookbook of the National Museum of African American History. In addition to providing delicious traditional recipes from Black communities all across America, the authors also talk about the historical and regional roots of Black food.

The Temptations. *Christmas Card*. 1970. Motown Records, vinyl LP.

This is the most important Black Christmas album of all time. Full stop.

Vandross, Luther. *The Ultimate Luther Vandross*. 2006. Sony Legacy, CD.
Now that you know about Fat Luther, it's time to listen to his velvet vocals. There's never too much Lutha.

4. WASH DAY

Good Hair. Produced by Chris Rock, directed by Jeff Stilson. 2009; Los Angeles, 2010. DVD.
Marcia cannot impress enough upon everyone the importance of this documentary in understanding Black hair and the impact European beauty standards have had on Black men and women's self-esteem for generations.

Vatican Council II. *Gaudium et Spes*. 1965. Vatican website, http://www.vatican.va/archive/hist_councils/ ii_vatican_council/ documents/vat-ii_const_19651207_gaudium-et-spes_en.html.
Gaudium et Spes tells us who we are as a Church and what our mission is. Why wouldn't you want to read it?

5. THAT CATHOLIC SHINE

Boff, Leonardo. *Sacraments of Life: Life of the Sacraments*. Translated by John Drury. 1987. Rpr., Portland: Oregon Catholic Press, 2019.
Boff reflects on the sacraments and the sacramental worldview in concise, beautiful prose. If you want a window into how to get that Catholic Shine, start here.

Francis. *Evangelii Gaudium*. 2013. Vatican website, http://w2.vatican.va/content/francesco/ en/apost_ exhortations/documents/ papa- francesco_esortazione-ap_20131124_evangelii-gaudium. html.
Pope Francis's apostolic exhortation *Evangelii Gaudium* (*The Joy of the Gospel*) is a handbook for how to find joy in Jesus and

how best to share it with others. Two out of two of us authors would recommend it.

6. REFINER'S FIRE

Bush, Edna Gail, and Natonne Elaine Kemp. *There Is Something about Edgefield: Shining a Light on the Black Community through History, Genealogy and Genetic DNA*. Rockville, MD: Rocky Pond Press, 2017.

Bush and Kemp write a novel-like exploration of their Black roots, genealogy, and genetics through the prism of life in their hometown of Edgefield, South Carolina. An engaging read for those who want to delve deeper into how Black families trace their roots.

Massingale, Bryan N. *Racial Justice and the Catholic Church*. Maryknoll, NY: Orbis Books, 2010.

One of the most important books in recent history on race in the Catholic context. Massingale connects the theological concept of original sin to slavery and institutional racism in America.

"Augustus Tolton." Archdiocese of Chicago website. https://tolton. archchicago.org/.

The Archdiocese of Chicago hosts a wonderful site dedicated to the life and canonization cause of Ven. Augustus Tolton. We love "Good Father Gus" and we hope you will, too.

7. IT LOOKS LIKE YOU'RE LEANING

While You Were Sleeping. Written by Daniel G. Sullivan and Fredric Lebow, directed by Jon Turteltaub. 1995; Burbank, CA: Walt Disney Studios Motion Pictures, 2010. DVD.

Find out more about Lucy, Jack, "leaning," the Ice Capades, and the time Joe Jr. had a barbecue in the stairwell.

Searle, Mark. *Called to Participate: Theological, Ritual, and Social Perspectives*. Collegeville, MN: Liturgical Press, 2006.

This short reflection on the liturgy by theologian Mark Searle talks about what "participation" at Mass really means—and how it transforms our hearts to know and love Christ.

8. MADE FOR SUCH A TIME

"The Book of Esther." *The Catholic Study Bible*. 3rd ed. New York: Oxford University Press, 2016.

If you haven't yet met Esther, you should.

Holmes, Barbara A. *Joy Unspeakable: Contemplative Practices of the Black Church*. Minneapolis: Fortress Press, 2004.

Holmes looks at how the spiritual practices within the Black Church have shaped its people and its history, enabling the Black Church to survive and thrive through the centuries.

Braxton, Edward K. *The Church and the Racial Divide: Reflections of an African American Catholic Bishop*. Maryknoll, NY: Orbis Books, 2021.

A powerful book from the recently retired bishop of Belleville, Illinois, about his experience as a Black man and Black bishop in the Catholic Church.

9. MY WHOLE BLACK SELF

Frey, Karianna, ed. *We Are Beloved: 30 Days with Thea Bowman*. Notre Dame, IN: Ave Maria Press, 2021.

Spend some time with Jesus and Sr. Thea Bowman in all her glorious wisdom.

Davis, Cyprian. *The History of Black Catholics in the United States*. Chestnut Ridge, NY: Herder and Herder, 1995.

The seminal work on Black Catholic history in America.

Cressler, Matthew J. *Authentically Black and Truly Catholic: The Rise of Black Catholicism in the Great Migration*. New York: NYU Press, 2017.

A more recent addition to the shelves on Black Catholic history, Cressler's book discusses the roots of Black Catholic communities in many Northern dioceses and the way the liturgical movement that flowed from Vatican II empowered Black Catholics to embrace their heritage and their faith side by side.

10. THE NECK OF THE CHURCH

My Big Fat Greek Wedding. Written by Nia Vardalos, directed by Joel Zwick. 2002; New York: IFC Films, 2007. DVD.
Find out what happens when the neck turns the head.

Rickard, Theresa. *Everyday Witness: 7 Simple Habits for Sharing Your Faith.* Notre Dame, IN: Ave Maria Press, 2019.
Sr. Rickard's eminently readable book combines stories and spiritual wisdom to help us all find our calling in the midst of our everyday lives.

Marcia Lane-McGee is the cohost of the *Plaid Skirts and Basic Black* podcast and a family teacher at Mooseheart Child City and School. She is a founding member, executive board member, and secretary of Catholics United for Black Lives and an executive board member and the vice president of New Wave Feminists.

Lane-McGee attended Benedictine University, where she studied English language and literature and minored in Spanish. She earned a national certification in Catholic youth ministry from the Center for Ministry Development and was certified in diversity, equity, and inclusion in the workplace from the University of South Florida MUMA College of Businesses. Lane-McGee previously served as coordinator of youth ministry for the Diocese of Joliet and the Archdiocese of Indianapolis, and as a community resource coordinator for Youth Guidance. She has been a guest on CatholicTV's *This Is the Day* and SiriusXM's *The Katie McGrady Show*. Her work has been featured in *Common Horizons* magazine and the *Catholic Herald*. She lives in the Chicago, Illinois, area.

www.psbbpodcast.com

Facebook: marciacenice

Twitter: @stylishlyCia

Instagram: @stylishlycia

Shannon Wimp Schmidt is cohost of the *Plaid Skirts and Basic Black* podcast and a founding member of the board of directors of Catholics United for Black Lives.

She earned a bachelor's degree in theology and Italian from the University of Notre Dame and a master's degree in pastoral studies from Catholic Theological Union. Schmidt has more than a decade of experience in youth and pastoral ministry and has served in various capacities, including director of RCIA, adult faith formation coordinator, diversity educator, interfaith ministry leader, and theology teacher. Her work has been featured on CatholicTV's *This Is the Day* and in *The Catholic Moment* and *Common Horizon*.

Schmidt lives with her husband, Eric, and their four children in the Indianapolis, Indiana, area.

psbbpodcast.com
Twitter: @teamquarterblk
Instagram: @teamquarterblack

Kathryn Whitaker is a Catholic blogger, speaker, and freelance graphic designer. She is the author of *Live Big, Love Bigger*.

AVE
AVE MARIA PRESS

Founded in 1865, Ave Maria Press,
a ministry of the Congregation of
Holy Cross, is a Catholic publishing
company that serves the spiritual and
formative needs of the Church and its
schools, institutions, and ministers;
Christian individuals and families; and
others seeking spiritual nourishment.

———◈———

For a complete listing of titles from

Ave Maria Press

Sorin Books

Forest of Peace

Christian Classics

visit www.avemariapress.com

AVE MARIA PRESS
Notre Dame, IN
A Ministry of the United States Province of Holy Cross